Self Approved™

A guide to accepting, loving and
expressing the person you truly are

by Kat Trimarco

contact@KatTrimarco.com
www.KatTrimarco.com

Tellwell Talent
www.tellwell.ca

ISBN
978-1-77302-564-3 (Hardcover)
978-1-77302-563-6 (Paperback)
978-1-77302-565-0 (eBook)

Dedication

For Keeth Evan Cherrington

I love you, hunny.

Contents

PART 1: A LITTLE ABOUT ME

PART 2: BE YOURSELF BLUEPRINT™

Introduction

Three years ago, I lost control of my life.

Everything crumbled around me.

I reached my rock bottom.

For the thousandth time I sat with my nose pressed against the back of a bar toilet, snorting back every speck of white powder I could see. I swiped my finger across the back of the toilet cover and vigorously began rubbing my gums. As my teeth and face went numb, my eyes rolled back into their sockets and everything turned black. That's the last moment I remember until I came to in my living room.

I was at home. That's my safe place... right? But how did I get here?

It didn't matter. I grabbed my purse and frantically rummaged through every zippered compartment. I knew my baby was in there somewhere. I knew I could escape once I found her. Go back to the other place. Where, for an elusive moment, my body would feel tranquil. Without pain. Which was maybe just the closest to feeling good I would ever come.

I couldn't find her though. My little white goddess all wrapped up snug in the corner of a zip-lock baggie. My heart skipped a beat. *What the fuck?* Where had she gone? I knew she was in there… At least a gram, maybe two… certainly more than enough to keep me paralyzed until the morning. Did someone take her from me between blacking out and now? Or did I snort her all up? Maybe that was why I couldn't clarify what had happened over the past few hours and how I had ended up here.

I searched high and low.

Nothing.

Desperately I scrolled through my phone, firing out messages to anyone who could bring me more.

No response.

My last resort… there was booze here somewhere. Vodka. It only took me a moment to find it. I grabbed the bottle, twisting off the little black cap, tipping it, closing my eyes and swiftly gulping back big full swigs.

The warmth trickled through my body, cell by cell. Sweet relief. My body eased into the bed, or couch, or maybe even the floor. I don't remember. I just felt as though I had melted and became one with it. Now maybe everything would be okay. If I could have stayed in that warm soft place forever, never waking, then I would have.

But eventually I did wake up to my situation and to *myself*. And that's why I'm writing this book, so you can as well.

***

I used to believe my life was a series of episodes dominated by one central theme—that of people abandoning me. In retrospect, my life has actually been a series of situations where I abandoned myself. Each scenario ended up with me feeling as though a brick had been flung at my head, knocking me off my feet, leaving me crumpled and broken on the floor with no one and nowhere to turn to but back to myself. The degree to which I betrayed myself always matched the degree to which I *found* myself—all building upon each other and leading me to where I am today and right now.

The blows became softer with each hit. Now I can get back up on my feet and back on track more quickly. When I waiver, I feel the discord *sooner*. The warning signs are subtle, but I read them like a flashing siren.

Kat Trimarco

This newfound awareness did not happen instanta-neously—it took training. It took ignoring the signs over and over again until something in my life blew up. Now the woman I am today, the real me, knows how to *observe* and *listen*. As the days go by I continue to practice and get better at it.

I've learned how to better read my own life's blue-print, to approve of myself, as well as be at peace with each experience I have. I follow that blueprint and no one else's. I understand that nobody else exists on my life blueprint or controls the route I take and that's *okay*. That's because other people have their own indi-vidual and unique versions. We cross, intersect, and even collide with one another while following our respective blueprints. That's how it's *meant* to be. All that matters is that we follow our own. When you *aren't* then life will show you. This will come in the form of subtle signs, which if ignored, start getting bigger and bigger until BOOM!... you have no choice *but* to make a change or continue to live with the internal discord that will only intensify, creating more dif-ficult struggles throughout your life, leading to deep misery and possibly even death.

I've written this book to share with you my experi-ences, and to show you how I worked through mani-fold challenges I believed would take me down.

This is a book to help you live within *your* own self—to be yourself and approve of *who you are*. To dismantle the layers you've built up around who you *really* are that society, family dynamics, past circumstances and traumas might have built up around you.

There's a profound truth within you and it's the only one you need to acknowledge... the truth of your authentic self, which is invariably hidden behind all the masks you've put on to protect yourself against this world.

To be responsible to yourself and to acquire happiness you need to disassemble the ideas of who you thought you *should* become and to reveal who you *really* are and who you long to be. I believe we build identities and personas based on the notions of what society, our families and friends expect us to be. They can be nice... they can make life more *comfortable*, but they aren't *real*. No matter how much you convince yourself, they don't represent who you truly are.

Most of us approach our lives in a counter-intuitive way. We build up our hopes and expectations of arriving at some final destination of fulfillment, happiness, success, love and connection, but sometimes the path we take to get there is difficult and occasionally treacherous and exhausting. This is because we attempt to follow in the footsteps of others rather than forging our own specific and unique pathway towards our goals, desires, and dreams.

I used to spend a lot of energy examining how other people lived—looking at what they had accumulated and built around them, seeing *them* being supposedly happy, and then attempting to replicate their formula for success in my life. Thinking that if I could just get what they had then I'd be fulfilled and would reach my destination. I thought all I needed to do was just manipulate my behavior, actions, and looks until I *arrived*.

Little did I realize that the people who had the apparent trappings of success and on whom I modeled myself, often lived shallow lives and hadn't developed the inner feelings of fulfillment, love and connection... the very riches for which I was unknowingly yearning.

That's how I operated for a long time. The past few years, however, have been the total opposite, consisting of a complete dismantling of all the illusions and masks I had given myself as an identity.

It's been scary. It's taken me *far* out of my comfort zone—not once but over and *over* again. I felt as though I was enduring an internal death. A death of the person I was. And I grieved it like a death. Slowly. One bit at a time. The identity I had created for myself fell away and broke down to reveal the truth of who I *really am*.

I knew these falsehoods had to die, and with them the old patterns, behaviors, belief systems and limited ways of thinking. Without the death of the old I couldn't have been reborn or allowed my innermost truth to *shine* and be the leading force to drive my life and the choices I make.

That's why I've written this book. I want to help you live the life you really *want* to live. To help you feel the way you deeply desire and long to *feel*. To help you cure that *hunger* for something *more*. To help you take yourself from a place of endless running on the wheel of life to a place where you actually feel *alive*.

I know I can't be the only one who has suffered. I can clearly see it and hear it when I look around or when I talk to my clients and friends. We're living in a world where happiness is an illusion and anguish is the paradigm… the *norm*. Where struggle is rewarded and ease is considered lazy.

We don't even call it suffering because people have just accepted that this is the way life is supposed to be. Anything to the contrary would be shining the light where no one wants to shine it. But that's what *needs* to happen. We've masked it under the title of "living." But the way a lot of people are doing it isn't living at all. We're ruled by fear, which acts like a dog biting at our ankles just to keep us in motion.

I wrote this book to help you, the seeker, to create and live a more fulfilled life that's *true to yourself*, even if those around you think your dreams are crazy or unachievable. I assure you it's quite the opposite. I wrote this book to help you move beyond your current circumstances and personal behaviors that are inhibiting your growth and evolution. I wrote this book to help you live the life you want to live and are *meant* to live—the life you have the potential to live, but aren't currently living. To help you return home to yourself no matter how many years or decades you may have been wandering.

In this book you'll learn how to reconnect yourself with Source, create a life that's reflective of who *you* are, and be introduced to practical tools to implement into your life.

I've separated this book into two parts—memoir and self-help. Part I, the memoir, is my journey laid out for you to give you a better understanding of who I am, where I've come from, and *how* I've developed the Be Yourself Blueprint™. It outlines my journey from external living, rejection and denial through to self-awareness. I also identified certain themes in how I was living my life and then noticed those same themes occurring in other people's lives. And from this place, I was able to create change.

Part 2 of this book is the Be Yourself Blueprint™, my seven-step process to lead you home to yourself and ultimately *to peace*. These processes, called The Layers, can be applied to your life *right now* no matter what stage of your journey you're in. Along with the breakdown of each layer, I'll be taking you further into my journey with specific stories and anecdotes that will help you further your own exploration and application.

I recommend you read this book from start to finish, starting with the memoir portion and working your way into the actual processes. My personal journey will help you understand the Be Yourself Blueprint™ in real life terms and circumstances. Read each process and then work your way through the self-reflection exercises listed at the end of each chapter in Part 2. These exercises are questions you can simply contemplate, but for the deepest effect, I recommend having a private journal alongside you to actual write your insights in. When we write things down, they become more concrete and tangible than when they are images floating around in our mind. Writing down your responses can also give you clarity that you won't get from merely swirling them around in your mind. Be sure to implement these changes *into* your current life circumstances. Information and knowledge without action is useless, so this is the most *important* aspect.

Because this book is written in my authentic voice, you'll come across the occasional swear word or phrase. This is how I talk in real life and, thus, how I also write.

My intention is to help you live a life led by self-love and to embrace the real you. My goal is to help you move from a place of hopelessness into a place of tuning into yourself and in the process allow the energy of the Universe to show up in your world so you can be comfortable with who you are. To embrace and love who you are.

If you're reading this book then it has found its way to you for a reason. You may have already been consciously or subconsciously asking for help and guidance, and your yearning and desires have led you right here. I'm assuming if you've been drawn to and are reading this book that you want to adopt a life of feeling good about yourself, your relationships, and your life. Pat yourself on the back and congratulate yourself for that! *I'm* applauding you for that as you ease into a whole new world of feeling good and looking good without the intense mental struggle. Welcome to a world of peace and tranquility!

May this book provide some answers for your life's questions. May it be a tool you apply *into* your life, day by day, to shape and mold it into what you desire it to be.

That's my hope. That's my prayer. That's my wish *for you.*

PART 1:

A LITTLE ABOUT ME

Chapter 1:

The Start of My Journey – Childhood

My parents, Chris and Bill, were both spirit-minded hippies who met at a commune in Colorado during the 1980s.

My mom was a young and free soul who left the busy city life of Toronto, Ontario, where she had grown up, to explore other lands, as well as her deeper self when she moved to the States.

My dad, who had grown up in crowded Chicago, Illinois with his three brothers and three sisters, also sought solace in the mountainous terrain of the Rockies. He always had a strong connection to nature and the land.

Smitten with each other, and falling quickly and deeply in love, they got married. Shortly after meeting, my mom became pregnant. Nine months later my brother Joe was born. Less than two years later my mom had another surprise growing in her belly... ME! At almost nine months and ready to pop, she and my dad moved to Nova Scotia where I was born on the winter solstice and shortest day of the year—December 21, 1988.

My mom gave birth to me in the tranquility of my Nana's home with nothing more than a midwife and her own breathing to get her through the physical pain. Years later my mom would describe my peaceful and calm exit from her body and entrance into this world. My Nana's house was large and rustic. It was located only blocks away from where the famous Bluenose ship docked in downtown Lunenburg. Years later the house was renovated into a quaint bed and breakfast. When I was a teenager, I had the pleasure of going back to visit and walk through the very building.

Without remembering the actual event of being born, I feel in the depths of my soul that I can remember the deep connection between my parents and me. The union between us runs deeper than our physical DNA—it runs into the sacred contract between our souls that allow us to learn and grow through our relationship here on Earth. On some level, I *knew* that despite the challenges that would later unfold in my life with our relationship, that I had chosen my parents in this lifetime.

As quickly as my mom and dad fell in love, they grew apart. Only six months after my arrival, they went their separate ways and divorced, leaving Joe and me in the primary custody of my mom with weekend visits to Dad's place. To this day, they've never shared with me the details of *why* they actually divorced and, to be honest, I've not thought to ask. Because they separated before I was old enough to remember, I've never pictured them as a couple. To me, my mom and my dad's lives were very separate, and having two parents with two different households was the normal for my childhood. In the first few years of my life it never bothered me. I liked living with my mom while at the same time I loved going to my dad's for weekend visits. That was until other partners came into the picture...

When I was about four, my dad remarried a woman named Lisa. My mom wasn't far behind—she tied the knot with my then step-dad when I hit about eight. His name was Stone, which ironically I came to discover suited his overall nature and behavior.

I didn't get along with my step-mom from the moment I met her. She was half Japanese and half Canadian, tall and lean with long thick dark colored hair. She was very natural, although not at all beautiful in my eyes. She had unshaved armpits, and a dress style somewhere between a mountaineer and a teacher—boring and dull yet seemingly practical. Her personal style seemed to match her personality—dull and unhappy. Before her appearance in my dad's life, I remember him being playful and full of life, yet she seemed to bring with her a dark energy that dampened the house with her grouchiness.

Having no kids herself, she seemed oblivious as to how to interact with Joe and me, and she treated us as if we were nothing more than the leftover baggage her new husband had lugged into their relationship because he had no other choice. She loathed us, and we quickly began to feel the same towards her. In addition to the tense relationship between us, it seemed she and my dad were always bickering. I noticed how critical and judgmental she was towards everything about him, how he acted, and the choices he made. I didn't like this one bit.

As time progressed, I began dreading the idea of visiting my dad not because I didn't want to see him, but because I couldn't stand being around her. During every visit, Lisa and I would get into fights. The tension between us was constant. I longed to have my dad back, but this never happened. I felt as if I was in continual competition with Lisa for my dad's attention and love—her neediness would always trump mine. I was always left questioning who I had to be in order to win my dad's approval. I craved his love, but it seemed as though there was nothing left of it after pouring it into his romantic relationship.

My dad and Lisa soon moved to Calgary—a city on the other side of Canada from where we lived. This meant our visits became fewer and farther between. Meanwhile, my step-dad, Stone, took a job in Japan when I was about ten years old. With little notice or warning, the four of us packed our belongings and flew across the world to make a new home for ourselves in Asia. I was excited about the adventure, feeling no attachment to our current home in Nova Scotia, but I knew Joe felt like his roots were being ripped out of the ground.

With an English speaking school costing more than $20,000 per child each year, my mom decided to home-school Joe and me for the duration of the year. Until then, Mom had struggled to make ends meet, and I could feel her relief at the financial burden being lifted after she married Stone. With her not working in Japan, aside from an infrequent English class she taught to a few Japanese women, she was dependent on him to provide for us. He made sure to remind us of this often.

While the opportunity to live in a foreign country at such a young age was wonderful, the dynamic inside our home wasn't. All living quarters in Japan were small, meaning the four of us were sharing a two-bedroom apartment with paper-thin walls. Almost every night, Joe and I could hear mom and Stone having sex, which often turned from moaning and groaning into a fight, escalating to full blown screaming matches before they finally went to sleep. This became the norm most nights. As an energy sensitive child, the behavior I observed between them affected more than my eyes and ears and left me with a shameful and scared feeling in my belly. I always felt on edge. As if there was a tension in the air that was so thick I could cut it with a knife.

About half way through the year, Joe and I were shipped off on a plane to visit our dad for a couple weeks who was now living in Lake Louise, a tiny ski village in Western Canada where he and Lisa worked. Part of me was relieved to get out of the apartment in Japan, but I didn't want to be so far away from my mom.

I'll never forget one particular morning during this visit. My dad's and Lisa's apartment was also quite small with only one bedroom, leaving Joe and me to set up camp in the middle of the living room. Joe slept on the couch, and I took the floor.

My dad came into the living room where Joe and I were sleeping. It was early—the sun was still hidden behind the horizon. My dad gently shook my shoulder, telling me it was time to wake up.

But why? I didn't understand. It was still dark outside. Where did we possibly have to be at this hour? I didn't respond to his shaking.

Again, he shook my shoulder, now fully rousing me from my slumber.

My dad made us a quick breakfast, and then whisked us out the door and into the truck. Even though I kept asking what was going on and where we were going, no one gave me a direct answer. I intuitively knew something was wrong. My stomach tightened and my insides trembled as the car drove out of its parking spot and down the road.

We pulled out of the small residential area in Lake Louise and merged on to the highway leading to Banff—a bigger main town about forty-five minutes away.

Finally, during the drive my dad told me what the heck was going on! We were going to school.

I was terrified. Panic-stricken. The drive seemed to last for hours.

"Why are we going to school?" I asked.

I'd only been home-schooled and Waldorf-schooled up until this point, so I didn't understand why no one had warned or prepared me for this abrupt change. I demanded answers as we drove—none of them were forthcoming. My foundations and support systems seemingly began to crumble from underneath me.

We pulled up at the school, protected by a metal fence, keeping the kids in the yard and the roaming elk from the nearby mountainside out. My heart continued to pound as my dad parked the car and led us through the double glass doors into the school. I don't remember much except for feeling overwhelmingly hot. Everything around me seemed blurry as my emotions swirled inside of me... confusion, betrayal, sadness, anger and fright.

I hadn't been into an actual public school since I was in kindergarten back in Nova Scotia a few years prior. My mom had enrolled me, but each morning I'd go to school with anxiety that would take over my whole body, sometimes leaving me begging and crying to be taken home or in a catatonic state.

I didn't want to be in that big school. I felt like I was an alien in a room full of humans. The terror I felt every day when I tried to go to school became too much and my mom kept me at home to be homeschooled. I felt so much more at ease and peaceful there with her.

Back at the school in Banff, I remember being taken with my dad into a little room that seemed much more kid friendly than the general office where a warm-natured woman greeted us. Even though she seemed to ask me endless questions about my past, I liked her, which was probably the only thing that made my dad leaving me there somewhat bearable. Once my dad had left and Joe had been taken to his classroom, this kind woman led me into my new classroom. Every student in the room watched me as I walked in and sat down.

I felt abandoned. Alone. Scared.

I wanted to talk to my mom on the phone. She would know what was going on. She would tell me, and she would protect me. Or so I thought...

That evening the phone conversation came and went, and was no solace. I still had no answers! My mom seemed calm on the phone despite what I was telling her, which only confused me further.

I hated that my life felt completely out of my control and in the hands of someone else.

We continued to wake up at the crack of dawn each morning and ride the school bus into the neighboring town. Joe seemed to make friends quickly. I'd see him running around and playing with them at recess. He'd be climbing on the jungle gym in the schoolyard, and the sight of him made me cry—the only familiar thing in a world that felt foreign.

Eventually, I made a few friends too, but I didn't feel they really understood me. I felt like an outcast and tried to just blend in as much as I could.

Some months later, my class and I were walking from homeroom to art class. The route took us past the main school office. The office was lined with glass walls, giving me a clear view inside as I walked by. I spotted something recognizable to me and *only* me. Something I obviously shouldn't have seen.

A bag. A big, poncho like, brightly colored, square-patched bag. A bag that belonged to my mother.

She was supposed to be in Japan! Could she be here?

My heart fluttered, my mind raced, and my stomach did a somersault.

Before I had a chance to lift my gaze higher, the single file I was marching in had moved past the office and was shuffling into the art room.

Was that her? It had to be—no one else had that distinctive purse.

But it couldn't be. My mom was in Japan. Thousands of miles away on the other side of the world.

But it had to be. No one else had *that* purse. I'd never forget that purse.

But it *couldn't* be.

But it *had* to be.

But it *couldn't* be.

My mind ran wild, stirring restlessly until finally there was a knock on the door to the classroom, which the teacher answered. I didn't need to be told... I knew it was for me.

The principal led me to the office where indeed, my mom *was* waiting.

Although part of me wanted to hold back, feeling like I couldn't trust anyone anymore, I ran into my mom's arms and gave her the biggest hug, which she lovingly returned. I felt free. Rescued. Saved. Yet *panicked* at the same time. Why had no one told me what was going on?

What I didn't anticipate was that I would spend the rest of the day at the local police station, being questioned over and over again by different officers about what had happened over the previous few months. I did my best to answer honestly, yet I had no idea what had even occurred. Why was *I* being questioned? Shouldn't *I* have been the one *asking* the questions?

The truth slowly unfolded...

Our visit to Dad's was supposed to be temporary, but he decided, without my mom's consent or knowledge, to register us in school and keep us in Canada rather than sending us on a plane back to Japan. My mom had flown out without his knowing to bring us back.

Joe ended up choosing to stay behind with my dad while I departed on a plane back to Asia with my mom to finish out the year. It was only once my mom, Stone and I moved back to Canada that the legal side of this case unfolded. My mom and dad had to go to court to battle it out and defend their respective sides of the story.

In the meantime my mom, Stone and I moved to Calgary, about three hours from my dad, Lisa and Joe.

A piece of me was left behind in the mountains. Joe had been my only companion when the arguments got rough between mom and Stone. And they did. They got much worse.

The fighting and yelling that had been regularly occurring in Japan now escalated and intensified. My home environment was filled with hostility, anger, and tension. Seemingly out of nowhere and without any provocation, Stone would fly into a rage, at which point he would smash ornaments and picture frames off the wall, punch holes through the drywall, and scream vulgar words at my mom. I would peer terrified and powerless through the crack in my bedroom door until he finished.

This became my normal. The fear. The yelling. The frenzy. I felt completely unsafe and alone.

A year later we moved from Calgary to an acreage outside of the small town of Westlock. Joe was forced to return to us because my dad was moving back to Colorado. With Joe back by my side, at least I had a confidante to turn to when Stone's anger boiled over.

Although Stone never physically hit Joe or me, we were often the objects of the tirades he directed at my mom.

One night, in the middle of one of his rants, he suddenly burst into my room as I lay pretending to sleep. He demanded I get up and follow him to the living room.

I stood there in my pajamas, stiff-legged, chin down, gazing at the floor. I was terrified, trembling inside with my emotions wavering between wanting to cry and wanting to fight back and scream at him. In my mind, I told myself that if I could just stay frozen like a statue and not let him see me break down, he would go away. He put his face inches from mine and began screaming at me, telling me how useless I was and how I was costing him thousands and thousands of dollars of his hard earned money, and what a piece of shit father I had.

There were three words that stuck—"useless", "worthless", and "undeserving." He would turn and spit on the ground every time he wanted to accentu-ate a point. Those words were more than words... they were daggers that pierced through my skin, into my heart, and settled into my subconscious, shaping the way I would view myself for years to come, through my teenage years and into adulthood. Then he returned to berating my mother.

One of Stone's rampages stands out most clearly in my mind when for the first time, his verbal abuse turned physical. He started shouting, and I couldn't bear it any longer. I sneaked into Joe's room for comfort. We felt safer together. We sat on his bed, knees drawn up to our chests, quivering and waiting for the screaming to stop.

Eventually, the fight between mom and Stone moved outside where it quickly worsened. Joe and I peered out of his bedroom window where we had a clear sight of them both. Stone continued to yell in her face and then we gasped in horror as his fist swung across and connected with her face. The blow knocked her to the ground where she sprawled unconscious across the lawn like a lifeless ragdoll.

Joe and I huddled on his bed, tears streaming and panic rising. Was she alive? Was she breathing? What were we supposed to do?

We watched Stone grab our mom, still unconscious and then throw her into the passenger seat of his truck before driving away.

Not knowing what to do or who to reach out to, my brother called my dad in Colorado who instructed us on what we should do next. We had to get out of the house. We ran out of the door, grabbed our shared dirt bike, and ripped down the gravel road as fast as we could to our twin friends' house where they lived with their grandma. Speeding away from the house, we passed Stone's truck parked on a turnoff just off the road. We dared not stop for fear of what we might see and what might happen to us next.

When we got to our friends' house, their grandma seemed relaxed and unconcerned about what had just happened. She sat us down at the table and continued to stir the chocolate chip cookie dough she was about to bake.

Some hours later, our friends' grandma got a phone call and we were sent back home. I felt the tightness around my throat and heart relax as we walked in to the house and saw my mom both alive *and* conscious.

No one spoke about what had transpired and, like every other fight they'd had, it was swept under the rug and not mentioned again. I was left feeling confused because this behavior was being treated as normal and okay. I knew it wasn't and the fact that everyone seemed to act like it was, made me trust them less.

Later that week, Stone took me out for ice cream. I felt nervous around him, like I was walking on egg-shells. I thought he was taking me out to talk about what had happened, but again the issue went unad-dressed. I felt in some way this was his way of apolo-gizing or trying to "smooth over" his behavior.

This episode left me with deep emotional scars. The images, the sounds, and the hostility burned into my psyche.

Finally, after years of enduring these angry out-bursts, this incident was the final straw for my mom. She worked up the courage to leave this monster, and the three of us moved to a little house just down the road from the acreage. She divorced him not long after. Every once in a while Stone would come by the house, turn into a raging lunatic, and try to break down the doors. Eventually, he moved away to the city and we never heard from him again.

I ran into him once many years later. I was a waitress at a local restaurant in the city. He sat down at a table with a large group of people and, while I wasn't the one serving him, I was asked to "run" food to their table. I trembled at the mere idea of it, but being the hard worker and obedient person I was, I dared not decline a work order. I walked right up beside him, and placed his plate of food in front of him. Our eyes connected. I don't think he had any idea who I was, and if he did, he did a fantastic job of hiding it.

"Thank you," he said, and returned to the conversation with the man beside him.

I didn't know how to feel or what to think. This time he had no power over me. A part of me wanted to have power over him just so he could see what it felt like, but the effort would have been useless. I laid it to rest and vented my emotions to the safety of my journal later that night.

Stone was gone, but his imprint remained in my life for a very long time.

Chapter 2:

The Next Few Years – Junior and High School

Over the next few years through junior high school I struggled to figure out where I fit in. I felt like an alien who had plopped down from outer space to disguise herself amongst the Earthlings. I wasn't of them. I didn't understand them. I had no idea how they made the decisions they did, but I made it my personal mission to blend in, and study and observe every move of my peers, who seemed to have it together. They clearly knew something I didn't, and I was determined to figure out what that missing link was.

Witnessing others' behaviors was how I made decisions and how I molded my actions, rather than following what felt good or natural to me.

Although at the time I couldn't put it into these words, I wanted love and connection and I longed deeply for acceptance. In my core, I felt an intense craving for the male attention I could never get from my father. This manifested as me trying to get attention from the males in my school. Somewhere in my mind at this young and tender age, I adopted the idea that men wanted sex and only sex and that if I could give it to them *then* they would love me.

My earliest experience was in grade seven. My brother was in grade nine and his class was going on some sort of extracurricular field trip to the waterpark in Edmonton. Each student's family was invited, so there I was hanging out with my older brother and all of his hot friends in our bathing suits at the pool. I was smitten with one friend specifically, and desperate for his attention, I started talking about giving blowjobs and having sex as if it was something I had experience in. I could feel the knot clench around my stomach as I pretended to be someone I wasn't in a needy attempt for acceptance.

This behavior escalated and magnified as I moved through junior high where I would go to great measures to get the attention of the older males in high school. Talking about sex and blowjobs led to *giving* sex and blowjobs, and little by little my self-respect dwindled.

I'll never forget my first sexual experience. I was thirteen years old. I met up with an older boy who went to a different school. He picked me up in his old beater car and we went for a drive, pulling over on the side of the road in an industrial area to swig back some drinks and puff on a joint. My head spun and my body relaxed. I liked the feeling. Every bit of tension slipped from me, leaving me feeling warm and cozy.

With the alcohol and weed pumping through our blood, our hormones took over. We ended up in the back seat with my pants on the floor.

Are we going to have sex? I wondered, as if it was a decision I had no say in.

He slipped his finger inside me, and a shooting pain ran up through my entire body. I thought this was supposed to feel *good,* but it was far from pleasurable. I dared not express the pain my body was feeling for fear of disappointing him. I closed my eyes and endured the probing, even forcing a moan every now and then, mimicking what I'd seen in porn as a sign of pleasure. This was what men *liked,* right?

After what felt like an eternity, he stopped and relief flooded over my body. I sat awkwardly, naked from the waist down in the backseat of the car as he proceeded to tell me he wasn't looking for anything serious or a relationship of any kind. I listened to his words but felt awkward sitting naked and exposed. I put on a brave face, but everything inside me collapsed. I dishonored my true feelings and agreed that I too wasn't looking for those things. Nothing could have been further from the truth.

Crushed. Humiliated. Unloved.

Before the conversation could go any further, we spotted another vehicle approaching us. He jumped into the front seat to speed away as I fumbled to find my panties on the floor in the dark.

This first sexual experience left me shattered and searching for *more*. Thinking something was wrong with me and that was why he didn't want a relationship only perpetuated me to prove myself in a bigger way, which led to many other similar experiences.

Later that same year, my mom flew to Toronto to visit her sister for the week, leaving my brother and me home alone, believing we were responsible enough to take care of ourselves and the house.

It was a Friday night and I was sitting at home texting my best friend on my pay-as-you-go black and grey Nokia phone—my first ever cell phone. I wanted to hang out, but she was out with her boyfriend at his friend's house where a bunch of them were drinking. My fear of missing out reared its head, but not wanting to invite myself over, I asked if she wanted to come over and bring her friends.

They arrived a short time later and before I had a moment to comprehend what was happening, a full-blown house party had broken out. My brother started shaking his head at me, telling me how much shit I was going to be in when Mom found out. In that moment, I didn't care. All I saw was the attention and popularity that would come my way as a result. I felt unstoppable and so cool, having all the older high school kids over, drinking and smoking. To top it off, I snuck away with one of the most popular guys in school, making out and exchanging oral sex with him in his car. I thought for sure this was my ticket "in."

"In" to what…? I don't even know. Acceptance maybe. Acceptance from others that I unknowingly was using to substitute for my lack of self-acceptance.

I soon found out my behavior had the exact opposite effect. When Monday rolled around and I walked down the school hallways the older high school girls started calling out "slut" and "whore" at me.

All I wanted was love, connection, and acceptance yet everything I was doing to attain those things only separated me further from them. The people whose approval I desired the most ended up being the ones who publically shamed me.

Feeling more and more disconnected and with my self-esteem quickly plummeting, I travelled further down a dangerous road of heavy drinking, drug use, and unprotected sex with men I hardly knew, let alone had any sort of emotional connection with. The attention they focused on me, no matter how temporary, felt like a small slice of heaven. It felt so good I longed to envelope myself in it. At the same time, I also believed it was impossible to live in this place for more than those few precious moments. It was like getting my "fix." I started to accept the shame that came after these encounters as the natural consequence of getting a few delicious moments of this so-called connection.

In my mind, I had to make these sacrifices just to come by the feeling of what I perceived as love. I wanted the feeling of mattering to someone. *Anyone.*

Along with my sexual promiscuity came lots of alcohol. It felt like the one thing that dropped the barrier I had built up around myself, protecting my heart. I felt good when I drank. It was like all my worries went away and I could be in that one moment. *Present.*

Occasionally, during lunch hour at school, a bunch of us would find someone to bootleg booze for us, and we'd drive out of town on country roads to drink until it was time to go back. Depending how much we guzzled would depend on *if* we went back to class or not. With a light buzz we could get away without the teachers noticing, but sometimes we'd be quite drunk, making the executive decision to skip the rest of the day.

One day after I chose to go back to class after such a lunch hour, I slipped in gym class on the stationary bike and busted my knee. My Phys Ed teacher sent me to the office to get my injury checked out. I trembled the whole way there, thinking for sure I would be caught being drunk at school, but I somehow pulled myself together enough to pull the wool over the principal's eyes, blaming my clumsiness for the accident.

This type of behavior continued, and when I had finished grade ten and my brother graduated high school, my mom decided to move us out of Westlock and into the city of Edmonton about an hour away.

It didn't take me long to find a peer group in my new school that were doing the same type of things. Only now, on top of copious amounts of drinking and weed smoking, I was popping ecstasy pills, smoking cigarettes, and inhaling nitrous oxide—a gas that causes dizziness and blackouts. Despite all the classes I was skipping, I still managed to hold myself together enough to graduate school and with good grades. I think because I held it together so well through all this self-destructive behavior, I had convinced myself that what I was doing really wasn't that harmful. I thought it was just part of being a teenager.

My mom was worried about how much I was drinking, even though she probably only knew the half of what was *actually* going on, and sent me to a therapist. I refused to open up to her and sat there with my arms crossed, laughing and being snarky in my responses to the questions she asked about my lifestyle. It didn't take long before my mom stopped paying for these sessions.

I was stubborn and this stopped anyone from being able to help me.

Chapter 3:

Lost and Insecure – Into Adulthood

I was living my life based on what other people wanted of me or, more specifically, what I *thought* they wanted of me. I followed this formula through my teens and into my early adult life. I didn't know and wouldn't have believed that people lived any other way. This was my version of reality. Figure out what people want of me then become that person—never mind the internal struggle this caused me. Anytime I did something I thought people wouldn't approve of, I'd dilute it into a likeable version of myself or omit it completely.

I soon discovered it was impossible to keep up with everyone's expectations because each person had different standards, criteria and values. I exhausted myself trying to analyze how I could gain approval of the multitude, and then did absolutely everything within my power to tweak and refine myself, depending on whose company I was in.

To many people watching I appeared to have it all together—aiming, striving, and achieving excellent results in school. I was trying to fit in with all the "cool kids" yet at the same time I was also determined to impress my teachers and parents, scoring honors throughout my high school education. I downplayed this to my peers because being too smart wasn't cool, instead it was considered to be nerdy. Nevertheless, I carefully balanced the two in an attempt to impress everyone.

I became an expert at figuring out whose approval I needed at any particular time, and like an arrow pointed at a target, I'd aim, shoot, and score. I mastered the skill of transforming myself according to how I wanted these people to see me. In that context, I was very successful in my life.

Even amidst the partying in high school, I still had ambition and my stubborn spirit couldn't keep me from anything I decided I wanted. One thing I knew I wanted to do was be a hairstylist. From as young as elementary school, I'd heard about cosmetology taught in high school where the students learned how to style, cut and color hair and actually practiced on real life clients in the school salon. I couldn't wait for grade ten to be able to take this class!

At the age of sixteen and in grade eleven when I thought I had enough schooling under my belt, I applied for a job at a high-end salon in West Edmonton Mall. I had a part time job since I was thirteen, but I wanted to step out into what I considered the "real" work world and start pursuing my passion. I always aimed high.

I waited and waited for the phone to ring for that job, but the call never came. Not wanting to accept this as my fate, a few days after applying, I called the salon and asked to speak with the owner. When I was put through to him, I explained I had dropped off my resume a few days prior and was calling to follow up.

"No!" wasn't a word I took in or heard very well, so when he said he wasn't looking for apprentice stylists at the time, but *was* hiring front end receptionists, I jumped at the opportunity.

Soon I was working in my then dream salon, answering phones, booking and ringing through clients. I also had a foot in the door for my future hair stylist career. While it might have looked like my life was on track in accordance with my dreams, behind closed doors and beneath the smile I plastered on my face every day, I was hurting.

Every weekend I was out getting absolutely shit-faced with my friends, oftentimes drinking more than a twenty-six ounce bottle of vodka before we even hit the bar. For some reason, this was the only way I knew how to socialize and make connections with people, feeling like it gave me a mask to filter through who I really was—it gave me a false sense of protection so that other people couldn't see how damaged I felt underneath.

While I worked my butt off at the salon, overachieving yet again to prove my worth, this still didn't stop me from strolling in every Saturday, feeling so hungover I could barely hold myself together. I think the only thing that *was* holding me together was my sheer determination to succeed and impress. I would slough off how horrible I felt physically and emotionally because I didn't want people to think less of me. My fear of failing kept me going.

Despite this desire to succeed, I'd often found horrible over-the-top excuses to call in sick on the weekends. Sometimes I'd wake up and the hangover was too much to cover up and I couldn't pull myself together.

On one occasion I went as far as telling my boss that my brother had fallen off a two-story building at work, was at the hospital, and going in for immediate surgery—something I'm *not* proud of, even to this day.

It didn't take long after graduation and stepping into the work world of hair styling that snorting cocaine became part of every weekend. Oftentimes it also seeped into my spontaneous weekday party nights.

At the time this behavior didn't feel extreme in any sense to me. Maybe because so many people I was friends with were doing exactly the same thing. Maybe I normalized it in my mind to the point I felt okay about what I was doing. In fact, I think it was a perfect harmony of both aspects... a symphony of surrounding myself with others who behaved the same to justify my own choices, as well as looking at these people and believing this was how the world and friendships operated.

I surrounded myself with people who were living a similar lifestyle to me, and convinced myself this was the way life was. But deep down inside, I knew something better must exist. Deep down inside, I knew I was capable of more, and I knew I wasn't living outwardly as the person I felt dwelling inside—my soul.

Still... years passed by with this behavior ruling my life. I felt like I was just getting by. I kept working as a hair stylist and making enough money to pay the rent and put food in my belly with enough left over to support my party lifestyle which led me right smack into *him*.

Chapter 4:

Him – A Love Like No Other

I met him at a local rock concert. He was like a beam of light at the bar. My eyes found him the second I walked through the doors. Tall. Tattooed. So fucking handsome. His gaze penetrated my soul. My knees trembled in his presence. His charm had my heart thumping. The words from his mouth were music to my ears.

Even more magical than my intrigue was the fact that he had scouted me out. *He approached me.* I couldn't fathom how such a beautiful creature would even *notice* me, let alone make me the center of his attention. We danced, we drank, and we flirted and laughed into the night.

He was the brother of a good friend of mine. I wondered how I hadn't met him sooner. I had to get closer to this man. I had to have him in my life. I wanted him. All of him. All the time. I managed to accomplish just that, although I didn't get the outcome I expected. I thought he would bring me bliss. Little did I know the exact opposite would happen. Yet, ironically, our relationship ultimately led me to free myself from the cage in which I had imprisoned *myself*.

His name was Keeth. He was the lead singer of a popular local heavy metal band and a successful tattoo artist. He had no shortage of beautiful women flocking to him, including me. I just wanted to be his number one.

After that first night when we met in the bar, my world secretly started to revolve around trying to become a bigger part of his. We exchanged phone numbers that night and, when I woke up the next morning in my apartment with his sister, groggy and hung-over, her warning was loud and clear. I can still hear her words ringing in my mind, "Whatever you do," she said, "Please, *please* don't sleep with my brother."

I didn't listen.

Even though I was eager to please, I simply couldn't resist this man, and shortly after her warning to me I had the opportunity to hang out with him. I'll never forget that night and the desperation that dripped from my love longing heart.

I was out at a good girlfriend's birthday dinner when I got the text from another friend—the friend I'd been with the night I first met Keeth. She was out drinking and hanging out with him and his brother. She told me to get my butt over there!

I didn't need to be told twice. I immediately approached my friend whose birthday it was, nervous she would be mad at me for bailing, and told her I had to go. She knew how deeply I was crushing on Keeth, so she not only accepted that I was leaving her dinner, but gave me the keys to her car since mine was at home. I rushed to the pub where he was.

Again, we spent the entire night drinking, laughing and flirting—our eyes glued to each other. Only this time our worlds collided. Or should I say our genitals. In a drunken stupor. Over and over again. And again. And again.

Over the next few years, we'd often end up wasted at the same bar together where he'd wow me with his good looks and charm, knowing exactly what to say to get me swooning and into his bed.

He epitomized my ideal mate at that time, and he offered me a taste of the acceptance and love I'd been deeply craving my entire life. I thought that what he was offering me was as good as it got, so I chased it—hungry for more. Time and time again, I ended up in his bed with little more than a stale, booze-soaked goodbye in the morning. I lied to him, as well as to myself by pretending I was okay with this being the extent of our relationship when I secretly desired *so* much more. I wanted to be his woman and him my man.

After a couple years of this cycle of partying and sleeping together, all the while in between relationships with other people, we moved in next door to each other. Yes... *directly* next door to each other!

A couple of his friends, who were also my friends, were renting a house together when one of them decided to move out around the same time I was looking for a new place to live. The timing couldn't have been more perfect. Within the same month I moved in, the house next door went up for rent. It turned out that Keeth and his brother were forced to leave their rental because the owner was selling the property, and they ended up moving next door. The timing couldn't have been more synchronistic.

Our bedroom windows almost lined up with each other. This excited me. Maybe now I'd get more from him than the occasional drug and booze induced lovemaking session. I wanted to be closer to him and here I was—right next door. If by nothing more than sheer proximity, we'd be sure to spend more time around each other. I loved the idea. I loved every-thing *about* it.

A few months after my move, we went on a road trip together to Calgary, a city located about three hours away, to attend a tattoo convention. He was working there and I was supposed to be attending with a friend when she bailed at the last minute. I was so disappointed and when I mentioned this to him in passing, he invited me to come with him. My heart leapt at the offer! It's like we were being set up to spend more time alone together, and my initial disappointment about my friend ditching the event was quickly replaced with elation that her absence had opened up the opportunity for me to spend the weekend with Keeth.

We awoke early and hit the road to Calgary, driving directly to the tattoo convention. At the last minute, his brother and another of our mutual friends decided to drive down separately and spend the weekend with us. That evening after the convention, Keeth and I raced to the hotel room for a moment alone before the others arrived.

We rushed in as the door slammed behind us. Ravenous for each other's bodies, he grabbed at my pants, pulling them from my waist and dropping them to the floor. He pulled my head to the side and kissed the tender side of my neck. My heart pumped faster and my knees buckled as he pushed me on the bed. With our shoes still on, he devoured me then pushed himself into me. I opened my body and my heart, letting him take me.

We barely had a chance to pull our pants back on before his brother and our friend arrived, barreling through the door. I wiped my lips and tried to play it cool, and pretended as if we hadn't just had a steamy quickie seconds before they walked in.

The tension and hormones between Keeth and I intensified as we went to a bar for drinks with a bunch of other artists and attendees who had been at the convention all day.

I'll never forget the moment he publically "claimed" me and how honored I felt—the moment I'd wanted for so long. I was talking to another artist, a man whom he worked with. We were drinking and laughing when Keeth came up beside me, wrapped his big arm around me and pulled me in close, nuzzling his face into my neck. I welcomed his advance by standing high on my tippy toes and planting a kiss on his cheek—an acceptance of his claiming me.

We ditched the party early that night and again snuck back to the hotel to make drunken love before the boys returned.

From the moment we returned home from that trip, I don't think I slept in my bed more than once or twice over the next year. I was with him almost every moment I wasn't working. I thought I had achieved what I desired. I thought it was the end of my journey of longing for love and that I'd finally feel complete. I thought *he* would complete me.

Nothing was further from the truth.

We were hungry for each other's bodies, but deeper than that I felt a hunger for his love. A hunger that felt unquenchable. A desire so deep in longing, I didn't know how to express it sober. I loved drinking with him because alcohol was the one thing that allowed me to drop my guard and open my heart. It was the only time I felt a false sense of safety to express my love.

I was addicted to love. Or maybe I was just addicted to the *idea* of love. Further yet, maybe I was addicted to chasing love in a man who was incapable of giving it to me—only a deeper reflection of my inability to love myself.

My tendencies quickly sucked me into Keeth's dark world. I thought once I won him I'd be secure. That I'd feel safe from the other floozies battling for his attention, but it instantly made things worse. Keeth's inner demons ran wild, and I couldn't tame him *or* them. No one could.

I didn't know just how dark Keeth's life was until I was sitting in it with him. Aside from our regular boozing and party favors, Keeth was using prescription

OxyContin, crushing and snorting it multiple times a day.

My first glimpse of this was during our drive home from the weekend in Calgary. We stopped on the way and met a friend of his in the parking lot of a convenience store—a friend I'd never met. This was a different kind of friend. A friend who was supplying. In that moment when I watched these grown men exchange a wad of money for a small bottle of pills, I didn't understand the scope of what I was witnessing, but I did know it made me feel uneasy. It made my stomach do a flip and not in the way it had the first time I met my handsome counterpart in the bar the night we first met.

Right there in the car I watched as Keeth dispensed two pills from the prescription bottle, crushed them on the car console, rolled a paper bill and snorted back the white powder.

I'd done a lot of cocaine while drinking and partying, but this seemed different. This was the middle of the day and we weren't drinking and partying but simply on our way home to enjoy a relaxing evening.

This was the first incident in a long year full of further ones that pulled me into the cyclone of Keeth's drug addiction.

I acquired a new mission, and that was to heal him. To convince him of his potential and to become all that I, as well as many others, saw in him. Little did I know it was easier for me to spend all my energy trying to change and improve his life than it was to look into my own shadows and live up to the life I was capable of, but not fulfilling. Somehow I believed if he could rise from the ashes, I would rise with him. I didn't comprehend this on a conscious level at the time though— looking back I can easily connect the dots.

I wanted to heal him. I *tried* to heal him. What I didn't understand was that on the deepest level possible, I wanted to heal *myself*.

This manifested in me trying to help Keeth overcome his addiction to drugs. The amount of oxy he ingested daily was enough to kill the average person twice over, especially since he often mixed it with booze and cocaine.

Hypocritically, every once in a while I would join him in crushing and snorting the little white pills. I'd never admit out loud how much I enjoyed it. It was like a warm bliss washing over my body... a blanket of love wrapping around me, cocooning me in safety. I felt more connected to him in those moments than any other. We'd sit outside, me on his lap, with his big gentle arms wrapped around me, as we'd smoke cigarette after cigarette together. We'd talk for hours into the night, lying in bed taking turns massaging each other's hands.

He was my best friend. I loved him so much and I would have done anything for him.

There were many nights he would cry, professing how much he wanted to get better—that he wanted to be free from the clutch the drugs had on him. Every call for help broke my heart. I wanted him to be happy. I wanted him to be the man I saw underneath it all, dying to come out and live a full life. And more than anything, I wanted him to love me and be able to receive my love. *I wanted it so bad.*

One morning after he'd spent the night sobbing to me that he couldn't continue living like this anymore, I had a light bulb moment! Racing to the computer, I typed in "*Intervention Canada Application.*" If we couldn't afford rehab for him, someone else could!

Intervention is a national television show that documents the life and struggles of an addict. Each episode features a different person. At the end of the episode, the family and a professional interventionist stage an intervention and the producers offer the addict immediate treatment into a rehab facility. Throughout the filming, the person suffering is told they're making a documentary, drawing awareness to addiction. They're *not* told about the intervention or the rehab on offer at the end of filming.

I knew a lot about Keeth and his family, so I was able to go deep into detail as I filled out his application.

After hours of typing, I hit the big red "submit" button and held my breath.

I refreshed my email every twenty minutes after that, anxious to hear back. My heartbeat doubled in pace into the next day and in less than twenty four hours when I hit that refresh button on my phone, there it was—an email from the assistant producer.

It stared at me, daring me to open it.

Hands trembling, I clicked on the message. As the email opened, my eyes darted all over the page, trying to take in every word at once.

They wanted him.

The producer wanted to set up a call with me and talk further. I could barely breathe as I replied.

Holy shit! They wanted him! They liked his story! This could be our ticket out—*his* ticket to *freedom!* My mind raced and my heart thumped hard. I didn't know what was more prominent, the excitement or the fear. How was I going to tell his family? Would they be on board or would they be mad at me for applying? This was, after all, a *national* television show. Everything would be exposed.

I didn't care. He needed help.

Setting up a time to talk with the producer was difficult because I was always with Keeth and by this time his youngest sister was one of my roommates in the house. I wanted to keep this private until I found out what was actually going to happen.

I scheduled the call for early one morning before work. I lied to Keeth, telling him I had an eye doctor's appointment. Then I drove to the mall and parked my car to take the call.

I answered every question they had for me to the very best of my ability. Fortunately, between my intimate relationship with Keeth, being good friends with his siblings and having a close relationship with his parents, I knew many details about his addiction *and* his early childhood life.

The producer explained to me that it was *utterly important* that he not know there would be an intervention involved—that this could make the whole plan crumble. I was to tell him it was a documentary and *only* a documentary. They would even send me emails under a different name, outlining the details of the documentary and what would be involved for me to show him. I didn't like lying and I wasn't very good at it.

She carefully explained to me that the next step would be for me to sit down with his immediate family and get them on board. They would also have to be interviewed and filmed for the episode.

I was terrified, but I knew I had to do this. When I got home from work that evening, I sent each of his siblings and his parents an individual text telling them I had an idea for us to help Keeth and we organized a get-together so I could outline the plan. Everyone except for his dad could make it because he was working out of town for the next couple of weeks.

The afternoon came, and my hands shook as I drove to the coffee shop to meet his family... I could do this... I *had* to do this. I closed my eyes, took a long deep breath, and stepped out of my car. I barely remember the next few minutes. My mind went blank, fear taking over.

After ordering drinks, we all sat down. My voice was shaking and my eyes darted around, unable to hold contact with any of them for more than a split second. I silently felt grateful for the sunglasses on my face—a shield hiding how scared I really felt.

I spilled it all out to them. I told them how deeply Keeth was suffering, even deeper than some of them were aware, to me applying for *Intervention* and what would happen moving forward with it.

It took some convincing from my end to get them all on board, but in the end they agreed, and that's all that really mattered. His dad, who was filled in later, decided not to participate in the operation.

The next few days, my conscience ate away at me as I boldly lied to Keeth. I followed through with the story the producer had for me about a documentary, and showed him all the supporting material they'd sent me. His eyes lit up as he talked excitedly about the impact his story could have to help other people from going down the same road he had traveled. A piece of my heart broke as I kept up with the lie.

There were still a few pieces of information I had to get in order for this to be successfully executed—I had to speak with his boss at the tattoo shop and his band manager. One afternoon Keeth left his phone in the car with me and I quickly unlocked it, looked up the numbers, and saved them in my phone.

Over the next few days, as we waited for the film crew to fly out from Toronto and interview all of us, anticipation mounted and my own tension became almost too much to bear. I couldn't lie any more. I couldn't handle looking my best friend in the eye any longer and giving him false information.

I made a decision. And that very evening, as I followed Keeth into the basement while he put a load of laundry in, I told him—*the truth*.

He was mad. Disappointed. And upset. *But...* he was still willing to go through with it, playing along through the intervention and going to rehab.

Over the next few days, together we watched an entire season of *Intervention Canada*, talking over and over again in depth about his feelings of going through with it. We devised a plan to cover his bills and financial obligations. All the details were lined up for this to work. And the best part of all—*he was on board*.

This could *really* be it, I thought. This could be what *saves his life*.

The film crew came and went, interviewing Keeth, each family member and me in depth, asking question after specific question about Keeth's life and how we felt about him and his using, unraveling every aspect of his life. They would take the footage back to the producer for her to make sure we all looked and sounded decent on camera.

Everyone's emotions ran high. This was happening. *It was really happening!*

Until...

I woke up one morning and opened my email inbox to find a letter from the producer, telling me she had received a phone call from Keeth—he had pulled the plug on the whole thing.

Suddenly, the few days prior started falling into place. Keeth had been pulling away from me physically *and* emotionally. I could feel him somewhere else. He was distant. He didn't want to hang out and had hardly answered my calls and text messages.

I could feel my heart thud to the floor and my stomach threatened to expel its contents as I saw our only hope, *his* only hope, walk out the door.

I tried. I tried everything in my power to get him back in the game and to convince him to follow through with this. He was having none of it, and I felt him slipping from my grasp like sand slipping through the cracks of your fingers when you squeeze it too tightly. He was gone. I could feel it.

I don't know what devastated me more—that he was walking away from the intervention or that I could feel him moving further away from me. I wanted him close, but he was somewhere else.

Keeth disappeared for a day, leaving me in panic and his family deeply concerned. He returned, only for me to find out he'd been staying at another woman's house where they'd been drinking and partying.

It was my breaking point. I felt betrayed and my heart shattered into a million little pieces. I was done. I couldn't do this anymore. I couldn't sacrifice my entire life pining for the love of a man I would never get. How could he really love me, let alone show it, if he didn't love himself? What I later understood was that I was the one not loving *myself*.

Chapter 5:

The Last Few Years – The Breakdown, the Transformation, the Recovery

The six months after Keeth and I broke up is best described as nothing less than a living, tortured hell on Earth. My entire life felt like it had been snapped in two. Any glimmer of hope of love was lost in the abyss of my own sadness, which was coated and masked in vodka, wine and blow. Every morning that I woke up was a harsh reminder of my reality. Waiting for the nightmare to be over, but it never seemed to end.

I did everything I could to escape from what I was feeling. I desperately tried *not* to feel. I partied and made myself get *really* busy. If I stopped, I'd have to look. I'd have to see what was going on. I didn't want to see and I didn't want to feel.

Various women would rotate in and out of his home from night to night. I'd see their cars parked outside his house and my stomach would flip. I'd lie in bed and would swear I could hear them moaning out his name in fits of pleasure. I wanted to die. I wanted to be anywhere but my own life. The pain was too much and I wanted to disappear.

One day I was unable to stay in the house any longer. I got into my car and drove. I had no destination in mind. I just drove. For hours and hours on end. At the point when I decided to return home, I stopped at a liquor store and bought two large bottles of wine. I pulled over on the side of the road to chug down the first bottle before driving home to slam the second. I was so consumed by my own emotion that the fact I was driving drunk and could've seriously injured or killed myself or others on the road took a back seat in my mind.

The irony of this situation was sublimely ridiculous... here I was drinking and snorting away the pain after desperately trying to push an addict into recovery. I'd never perceived myself as an addict and I still don't really identify with having been *addicted*, but the fact that I couldn't bare to feel my own emotions and was running away from them through drinking and snorting couldn't be ignored. It was as if life was holding a giant mirror in front of my face, reflecting all my own dark shadows back to me.

Living next door to each other allowed me nowhere to run and hide. Something was staring me in the face—something big. I spoke to my mom on the phone one night and during that conversation I told her I couldn't run away. I had something major to learn and would do whatever it took to figure out what that was. I wouldn't run anymore. I couldn't hide and, try as I might, I couldn't escape the painful feelings.

The breakup changed my life. It was the catalyst. It was the breaking point. It was my Divine storm. My rock bottom. My thud to the floor. I had nowhere to go but up. I had to go up.

I had to.

My rock *hard* bottom came on the night of my 24th birthday. Like every other night out, I had friends over to pre-drink and get ready. All of us girls, trying on our best outfits, curling our hair, and darkening our eye-shadow. Sometimes this was the most fun part of my night. Right when the first few sips of vodka would start to reach my bloodstream. I could feel my face flush red and my insides start gently tingling as my mood lightened and heightened. I'd start to get extra chatty, sharing stories and gossiping with my girlfriends.

I always felt the most connected to people during those times—the times before I was completely drunk and sloppy. Looking back, I think that's the only way I knew *how* to really connect with people. My tender heart felt so closed off—hidden away in protection mode, using booze as the only way to let down my guard and let people in. When I was sober, I was terrified to show who I was. So scared of being hurt—an even deeper fear that there was something wrong with me and that people would reject me if I let them see me.

So I kept myself hidden. Diluted.

The night of my birthday, I felt rushed getting home from work and getting ready to head out. Eating dinner took a back seat to the pre-drinks and prepping to look good, so off to the bar I headed on a mostly empty stomach.

Caught up in the excitement of celebrating my birthday with all my closest friends, I also barely ate at the lounge and dove right into drinks and shots.

Two of my girlfriends and I pitched together to buy a couple grams of coke. I always felt uncomfortable buying the stuff. I preferred situations when it would just magically show up like the times when I'd go to the bathroom with a friend and she'd pull a baggie full out of her purse. I didn't like being part of the illegal transaction of trading money for drugs. It somehow made me feel extra ashamed of my behavior.

However, on this occasion and as if this request had been spoken out loud, a few minutes after buying the first few grams, one of my friends came up to me on the dance floor with a birthday card in an envelope. She whispered in my ear, "Happy Birthday, Kat! Don't open this around people." I honored her request and waited until I was in the privacy of the bathroom to open my goods. Shoved in between a birthday card was another gram of coke. Surely I had more than enough now to keep me feeling numbed out for the rest of the night.

That was the last thing I remembered before waking up at my house some hours later in the early morning. For the life of me I had no memory of how I got home and what had happened between the hours of opening that card in the bathroom and returning to conscious awareness.

The worst part was that I felt half sober again. It didn't feel good. I didn't want to be in this state. And I didn't want to be back at home. I still wanted to be out having fun and forgetting my pain. Home was the place I associated with the most pain.

But here I was. In my living room, half of my birthday blanked out in my memory. I slammed back the remaining poison in the bottom third of a vodka bottle—just enough to make me pass out again. A part of me hoped I wouldn't wake in the morning. The bigger part of me *knew* I would wake to the exact pain I had been trying to drown out for months with it somehow only intensifying after every weekend binge.

When I woke up the next day, my anxiety was horrific. It seemed to worsen with each hangover I experienced. I felt uncomfortable in my own skin like I just wanted to crawl out of my body. I wondered if everybody felt this depth of pain when they went through a break up. I also wondered how the hell people survived divorces after vows of commitment and decades of a life together.

I called my mom the next evening after my birthday party, still battling intense anxiety and emotional sadness. I was supposed to be heading out to a friend's place for more drinks that night, but I couldn't seem to remove myself from the couch and the paralysis I felt in my body and emotions.

I told only half of the truth to my mom as I sobbed about how anxious I was feeling, proclaiming I didn't know what to do and I didn't know how to handle it. What I didn't tell her is that the anxiety was almost surely caused by the excessive amounts of drugs and alcohol I had consumed for the better part of the prior night—my lie lingered in the back of my mind, threatened to come forth.

I then called my friends that I was supposed to meet and told them I wouldn't be able to make it. In that moment, I got real with myself.

Really fucking real.

As I went to bed that night, I decided I wouldn't drink anymore. Somewhere within me, on the other side of my pain, was a voice that told me I couldn't continue like this. That the pain I was feeling would only worsen the more I tried to numb it.

It's like I was staring at a fork in the road. One path was familiar and well worn but littered with garbage and sludge—darkness lurking in every corner and ditch. The other road was foggy—I couldn't see where it led. All I could see was that there were many obstructions along the way. Boulders in the path, weeds growing everywhere. I would have to remove each block one by one to travel down this unsure road, traversing my way and figuring it out as I went.

They both seemed like kind of shitty options to be honest. I wanted to bypass the boulders and weeds and just be on the other side, happy, fulfilled, and carefree. That path, unfortunately, wasn't an option. I had to go *through* to get *to* my destination.

The foggy road was full of uncertainty. However, I stepped into the unknown with an *inner knowing* that it had to lead somewhere better than the black road I'd previously been traveling. I had to at least *try*.

For the next six months, I abstained 100% from all drugs and alcohol. I quit smoking cold turkey and dove head first into bettering my life, doing the best I knew how from where I was. I hired a personal trainer and started going to fitness boot camps multiple times a week that were located on the opposite end of the city from where I lived. This helped me stay out of the house and kept me occupied so I wasn't constantly wondering what Keeth was doing next door.

I ditched the fast food and pizza I binged on every weekend and traded it for lots of whole foods—fruits, vegetables, and homemade, healthified goodies. I discovered I had a passion for baking—taking healthy ingredients and making different desserts and baked goods. I set my alarm early every morning and drove to the gym for a workout before heading to work for the day. On the weekends, I'd spend an afternoon grocery shopping and prepping all my nutrient rich meals for the week.

My body started changing and I liked both what I saw and how I felt. These changes are what motivated me to keep going and kept me away from going out to drink and party on the weekends. I had never actually felt this good before, and I wanted to maintain this newfound way of being and feeling full of energy.

Every week when Friday rolled around, I'd tell my roommates and friends I wasn't drinking. It felt weird to be the only one left out from the group, but I was determined not to give up. Ultimately, I was determined to feel better and I knew walking away from this old lifestyle was the only way out. I vowed to get comfortable spending time in solitude with myself and committed to this vow.

Naturally, it didn't take long before I felt extremely disconnected from my friends. Truth be told, we didn't have much in common other than our partying, and our self-sabotaging behaviors and lifestyles quickly became apparent to me.

I remained isolated because it was the only way I knew how to stay focused. I didn't have a support system of people who were also living a sober lifestyle. In my own circle, I was the only one making these new changes and so it very much felt to me like I was the only one in the *world* living like this. This obviously wasn't true, but from my perspective at the time, it certainly *felt* true. Looking back, I can see how deeply it would have benefited me to reach out for more hands-on support, and indeed this is the route I'd recommend to anyone who wants to make a life change.

During this time, I dove into reading a plethora of self-help books, attending personal development seminars and taking self-growth courses—everything I could get my hands on that talked and taught of self-love and improving life circumstances. *I'd figure it out.* I'D. FIGURE. IT. OUT. I was determined.

Before long, it seemed I'd find exactly what I needed to read at precisely the right time. Books would find their way to me. Teachers, mentors, and courses would 'appear' right when I needed to hear what they were teaching. The Universe was leaving me a trail of breadcrumbs. Each time I thought I was completely lost I'd find the next crumb. I just kept following the path, still not knowing where it was leading, but knowing it was better than where I'd come from.

I kept going.

Six months after I stopped drinking, one of my best friend's birthdays rolled around. She had planned a big camping weekend trip about an hour and half outside of the city. All her friends and family were going and I knew exactly what the weekend would entail—everyone getting absolutely piss drunk.

My anxiety stirred in the pit of my stomach as I contemplated what to do. I wanted to go and celebrate my friend's birthday with her. I wanted to be social and have fun but truthfully didn't really know *how* to without booze. I didn't particularly *want* to drink yet I didn't know how I would handle being out there with everyone and stay sober. I wasn't fully confident in my decision not to drink—a decision that opposed the choices of my peer group.

I decided to go, driving out for only one of the two nights by myself and not bringing any booze. My mind raced during the solo drive. Back and forth... would I drink? Or wouldn't I? I hadn't officially declared a sober lifestyle at this point, but I was feeling good abstaining and I wanted to keep going in this new healthy direction. The other part of me was scared of losing all my friends and the life I had with them. They were really the only community I had at the time.

When I got out to the camp area, I was disappointed to see that half the crowd was already drunk and the sun hadn't even gone down yet—my friend the drunkest of them all. How could I judge? I had been exactly in her shoes just six months prior at my own birthday party, as well as many times before. Yet, here I was, not feeling like I fit in, and despite my best intentions—judging.

As the sun set behind the horizon and the campfire took charge of providing light, I continued to con-template whether to drink or not. After hours of agonizing and stuffing my face with snacks to stay occupied and avoid my feelings of angst, I poured myself a drink. And then another. And another... and another.

I thought I would feel sweet release. I thought I would slip right back in with my old circle of friends, par-tying and having fun. But I didn't. Even with vodka back in my bloodstream, I'd become a different person than I had been just six months prior. Instead of slipping back into my social, chatty, and fun drunk self, I was still analyzing my surroundings now just through a fogged veil and *still* feeling disconnected from my friends. I wanted to feel good, but instead I just felt gross. And then I got sick. Really, *really* sick.

I spent the rest of the night doubled over a plastic pail in my friend's camper, heaving until there was nothing left in my stomach to expel, and then heaving some more. All night and into the next morning and afternoon—cold sweating, holding my stomach as I tossed and turned on a tiny cot wedged in the corner of the camper.

It wasn't until after 2pm the next afternoon that I finally emerged from the camper and drove home. A solid hour and a half drive home alone—time to get really clear with myself about the decisions I'd made and the decisions I intended to make moving forward.

I sit here writing this, almost three years to the day I made that drive home. Almost three years to the day since I took my last ever sip of alcohol. On my way home that afternoon, I made a decision that has since changed the entire trajectory of my life.

Sobriety.

With this decision came so much more than abstaining from drugs and alcohol. With this decision came a choice to come home to myself. To look myself in the mirror and get really fucking honest—a decision to face every uncomfortable situation and emotion in my life head on and to walk directly into the fear I'd spent so many years running from.

I'm forever grateful for that night out camping, the sickness and all, because without it I wouldn't have gained the clarity I needed about wanting a sober life. I'd been sitting on the fence for the six months prior to that—not fully owning the direction I wanted to take with my life. Not fully stepping into who I wanted to be. And *that* was where the real challenge started. Getting sober wasn't the difficult part.

Being myself and liking myself was.

I started looking around at every part of my life—observing *how* I was living, *who* I was spending my time with and taking serious *responsibility* for my own actions and choices. A life previously based on victimization and blaming others for my circumstances now taken consciously into my own hands. I'd read enough new age spiritual books to know in theory that I created my own life, and that I had the ability to create beyond my current circumstances. Yet, until then, I hadn't actually been taking those ideas and putting them into practice. I hadn't been *using* the tools I had been learning to make the life for myself that I desired.

At first, I don't think I even knew *what* I wanted out of life. At least I hadn't actually put it into words and

owned it. Instead I'd just been angry and frustrated that I felt so stuck and powerless.

I finally started to understand through living it that I couldn't get to where I wanted to be without first knowing exactly where I was standing and from there getting clear with myself about where it was I *wanted* to be.

It felt like a "holy-shit" moment that lasted for months. Of course I felt miserable, sad, and unfulfilled because I was standing in my current life, not liking it... not feeling good about myself, who I was, or how I looked, *yet...* I had never really gotten clear on what it was that I really wanted let alone made much effort to move in that direction. I think I knew what I wanted deep within my being, but hadn't consciously articulated it into words.

Furthermore, I didn't feel *worthy* of anything better than what I was living. That was the most difficult part to undo within myself—the feeling I didn't deserve what I wanted. I had craved a more loving and intimate relationship, but I hadn't felt it was possible for me to have and I didn't really feel like I deserved it either. The same thing was true for wanting to love my body and feel healthy and energetic in it. I knew I didn't feel good in my body and had spent so much of my life fighting with my body in the silence of my own mind, but I hadn't really stated how I wanted to look and feel, let alone take action to get myself there.

Over the next three years since leaving my relationship and getting sober, I've lived into the truth of who I really am—who I really was all along but who hadn't been expressing. The person who was hidden away, waiting for society to approve of me as a precursor to approving of myself.

What I spent the next three years learning and practicing was that before *any* person could really approve of me and before I would feel accepted by society for every ounce of who I was and *am*, I had to first become self-approved. I could fight, kick and scream against every other person and situation outside of myself, trying to manipulate and control my outside circumstances until I was blue in the face, but until I took control of my own internal world and made my relationship with myself the primary focus of *all* my relationships, I would forever feel stuck—tires spinning in the mud.

Not anymore. It was a new era. An era of truth telling and truth seeking. Looking in the mirror and getting honest—honest with myself about how I was living and how I wanted to live.

My self-improvement and *approval* became the beacons that guided my every choice and every action, tuning out the voices, including my own, that said I couldn't live *exactly* the life I wanted to and feel the deep grace of fulfillment and peace that my being cried out for.

Self-approval.

I now live a life beyond what I could've fathomed only three short years ago, and it only continues to get better and *better.* I'm surrounded by people I didn't believe existed when I was living my old life. I've experienced the manifestation of abundance I thought was only reserved for an elite few—abundance in all of its forms, not just money. Abundance of love, health, time, peace, fulfillment, pleasure, friendship, and connection.

I've traveled to countries all over the world, exploring different facets of this planet and its people, experiencing first-hand how different cultures live. I've also explored the depths of my inner world, feeling out who I am, what brings me pleasure, and what my purpose is in this lifetime, as well as doing everything I can to live my best life possible, teaching and helping others to do the same. It was almost as though everything from my previous life *had* to crumble and shatter from the weak foundation it was built upon, so I could rebuild solidly. Rebuild from a place of truth. *My* truth.

My life now is a far cry from what it used to be. In only three short years since getting sober and choosing differently, I look back and barely recognize the girl I was. The weird thing is that I always *felt* like who I am now was the exact person that was hiding out on the inside of a very frightened girl. The only way I can describe it is that I had a *knowing* deep within my soul that this is the woman I was meant to be in this lifetime. I just had to remove the layers that were preventing her from coming out to play.

That's the disconnect we often don't see—the space between who we *really* are on a soul level and who we're showing up as. The choices we're making are oftentimes ones that don't serve our greatest good and don't serve us feeling or having all that we're capable of feeling and having. Yet, because it's who we are on a *being* level, it can be difficult to understand where the gap is and why our outside circumstances aren't reflecting the goodness that's inside.

The past three years for me have involved a peeling away of all these layers that were crusted and covering that *being* part of me—the truth of me. I got tired of all the effort and exhaustion that came from trying to be someone I wasn't—of trying to prove my worth to everyone because I couldn't see it myself. I wanted to get honest about who I was and drop the façade, not just to the outside world, but the façade I maintained to myself.

I got honest with myself about the shitty choices I had been making that left me wondering why my life wasn't what I deeply desired it to be but most importantly I took *responsibility* for where I was and where I wanted to go. Previously, I'd just been more or less coasting along and letting outside circumstances and people decide my fate, using these people and situations as scapegoats for the disempowering choices I myself was making. It was time to take my power back by recognizing that I did, in fact, have the power within the context of my own experience. And to be honest, at first I didn't even fully believe it, but all the books I was reading and all the seminars I was attending were repeating this to me over and over again. Surely if all these "experts" were saying the same thing, it *must* have some validity.

I was seeing that the way I wanted to feel, at peace with myself and my life, *was* possible, and knowing this was possible even if I hadn't experienced it, is what kept me determined and what kept me seeking.

I dove head first into health and fitness, using moving my body as my means of releasing emotions that I'd previously bottled down inside with booze and drugs. I took the energy I'd been using before to self-destruct into improving myself—I wanted to become the best version of me.

Throughout the second part of this book, I'm going to take you through the exact steps I took to change my circumstances and fall in love with myself for the first time. In these pages I'm going to take you from seeking approval outside of yourself to living a life approved of by *you*.

I'm going to take you on a journey of building yourself a solid foundation from which to craft the rest of your life. A foundation so strong it can weather any storm and not take you down. A foundation that will help you manifest the body you desire, the love relationship you dream of, and the crafting of a purposeful life. This is a foundation that will bring you a deep inner peace you might have only imagined up until now—a profound depth of self-acceptance, as well as acceptance of other people and circumstances.

I want to take you on a journey from self-loathing to self-love, from unworthiness to "I am enough," and from low self-esteem to bubbling confidence. All this and *so* much more is possible for you. In truth, it's your birthright. Most of us just weren't taught this—we weren't reminded of the powerful spiritual beings we are and the immense beauty in our own unique individuality.

Consider this your reminder. I say reminder, because deep inside your soul, you know this to be true. In the same way I felt like an empowered and confident woman long before my outside world reflected it, we're going to reawaken the greatness within you that might have been dormant until now.

It's time to wake up.

In the next section of the book, we're going to dive in deep and explore how to become self-approved. This is where I'm going to break down the seven specific processes I used to transform my life, and *still* use to create my life from the inside out.

Alright then... let's get to it!

PART 2:

BE YOURSELF BLUEPRINT™

Chapter 6:

Housekeeping – What You Need to Know to Get Started

Until now, I've been telling you my story, sharing where I came from and what broke down the façade of the life I was living and what cracked me wide open. I talk about these experiences and pains not to dwell in them or to *use them* to define who I am. I use them to help articulate how absolutely beautiful every single thing that unfolds in our lives really is, as well as how perfectly our individual experiences push us forward into the people we're capable of being if we choose to see it as such. I use my stories to teach and to help others make the transition from outside approval to self-approval because I absolutely know without a doubt in my heart that if *I* can make this shift, it is possible for *anyone* to make it.

I use my stories to articulate each process, which I refer to as The Layers in this section because theories are essentially useless if they can't be understood and applied to real life. It's my highest intention in the writing and sharing of this book to be real, raw and vulnerable with you. There will probably be many times you see yourself or parts of your own life within my stories if you haven't already—that's exactly why I share them. To bring light to the understanding that we're all connected. That my pain is your pain and my healing is your healing and vice versa.

I'm going to take you deep into the exact steps I applied to make the transition from where I was to where I am now.

The outside changes I've made have been obvious to those who know me. I'm happier. I'm more at peace than I've ever been.

I've traveled solo to countries all over the world when previously I was too terrified to walk into a restaurant alone. Now, I'm surrounded by love where I was previously surrounded by fear and co-dependency; connection and intimacy where I used to feel isolated and lonely. These are the feelings—the internal experiences only I can really articulate having transformed.

But they're what set up all the external shifts—what has attracted all the abundance and richness into my life.

There are a few principles I want to cover before we dive into peeling back The Layers. Forces working in our subconscious life are constantly affecting the life we live, but for many of us, have never been explained. Knowing these principles will help you understand certain things throughout the rest of this book—giving you both a deeper understanding for yourself and for *life* here on Earth. Understanding is one of your greatest powers.

Invisible Forces and Beliefs

The physical world you observe is only a small fraction of the Universe. This is a microcosm of the macrocosm. We're taught there's nothing else going on in this world other than what we can experience through sight, hearing, touch, taste, and smell. If you can't physically observe it via one or more of your five senses, then it isn't real, right?

WRONG.

The physical world that *can* be observed through our senses is amazing. It's beautiful. It's majestic. It's a miracle within itself. But it's only a small part of what's *actually* going on. It's a *reflection* of what's going on *within* us. Internally. Energetically.

Let's repeat that again so you can really absorb the importance of this statement…

The physical world we live in is a *reflection* of the *internal* world *within* us.

Why is this important?

Great question!

This is so important because most of the world is operating from a place of trying to manipulate and control outside circumstances and people through *force*. This is one way to create change, but it comes at the great expense of pressure, stress and working against the natural order of the Universe.

Because our outside world is a reflection of our internal world, we can use our lives as a mirror reflecting us back to ourselves, giving us clarity on where we can improve or make changes. By making changes on the inside, within ourselves, our outside world will, over time, rearrange, shift and change to match this new internal world we have created.

That's the big "secret." That you're not powerless to your circumstances. You're not stuck where you are because where you are right now is nothing more than a reflection of your internal world—your thoughts and feelings. In fact, your thoughts and feelings are one of the only areas of life that you actually *have* control over, and so, this is where your power lies.

Understanding this helps you to take your power back, and is simultaneously a call to step up and take responsibility for yourself and the life you are living *right now*.

The second important force to understand is the Force of Life. Besides being physical entities, each and every one of us is also an energetic being. There is an energetic world that's just as real as our physical world, only we can't interpret it with our usual senses. It's not dense enough to see and touch. It can be felt though.

It's the energy field that all of us originate from and the field we'll all return to when we're done with our bodies. It's what is pumping through every living thing on this planet. It's the part of us that seemingly "leaves" when we die.

I call this energy: Source, Spirit, the Universe, our Inner Guide, Intuition, Your True Self, and God. It's a force so large that it cannot be simplified to words. Nothing can capture the fullness and infiniteness that is this force. It's what operates our entire world. It's what you're made of. It's in every single thing that inhabits this Earth and everything beyond into what we can feel, sense and just *know*.

Our mind and ego separates us from this Spirit and can leave us feeling helpless and powerless to make a difference in our lives or this world. Many spiritual texts and teachings encourage us to abolish our mind and ego. While I've seen and felt the benefits of this viewpoint, I want to bring your attention to a different viewpoint where we *use* our mind, personality and even parts of our ego to live in complete *fullness*—that is, a space where mind, body and soul come together in harmony.

The Invisible Laws

Another important concept that's essential for you to be aware of before embarking any further on this journey is to know we're living in a *law-based Universe*. I'm not talking about traffic laws or any other government or man-made laws, but the only actual *real* laws that govern all aspects of this physical and non-physical world.

These laws are described by many great authors and spiritual teachers including, but not limited to: Esther and Jerry Hicks and the Teachings of Abraham, Rhonda Byrne in her famous book *The Secret*, which was also made into a movie, and Wayne Dyer in all of his award winning books.

These laws are as true and concrete as the Law of Gravity, even though you cannot physically *see* them. They govern our entire world, and if we just knew how to work with them then things would flow so much more smoothly and effortlessly within our lives. Instead, most people try to create change only in the outer layers of their lives instead of working with the laws and shifting their energy and focus to their internal world. Change on the internal level inevitably creates change in the external—it's just a much more efficient way of creating lasting change. The law you need to be aware of in this book specifically is the Law of Attraction.

The Law of Attraction

Simply put, the Law of Attraction is a magnetic power that draws what you consistently think about towards you. It draws to you what you vibrate energetically out into the world. Because we're energetic beings, we emit an outward energetic frequency that in turn, with no conscious effort, draws to us the equivalent energy. This determines the people, places, events and circumstances that show up in our lives. Again, the external is a *reflection* of the internal.

Throughout this book I'll often refer to the Law of Attraction in terms of setting intentions, so you can attract certain people or situations to you, as well as manifest the life you want. By understanding the Law of Attraction we're better able to understand why our lives are as they currently are, and we're able to regain responsibility and control over how and why our world is unfolding, as well as to begin working as a co-creator with the Universe on our life plan. It can also give us a fresh perspective that life isn't just completely *randomly* happening to us.

You can leave your sense of powerlessness in the past. Many of us have been taught to control (or attempt to control) the physical aspects of the outside world. Change on this level requires great force and effort... far more than is required. If we can learn to create change energetically, our lives will simply begin to *flow*.

I'd like to borrow the description of this law from Esther and Jerry Hicks and the Teachings of Abraham, whose books and videos have mentored me through much of the transformation in my life. They eloquently describe the Law of Attraction in the following way:

> *Everything in your life and the lives of those around you is affected by the Law of Attraction. It is the basis of everything that comes into your experience. An awareness of the Law of Attraction and an understanding of how it works is essential to living life on purpose. In fact, it is essential to living the life of joy that you came forth to live.*
>
> *You see the Law of Attraction evidenced in your society when you see that the one who speaks most about illness has illness; when you see that the one who speaks most about prosperity has prosperity.*
>
> *As you begin to understand — or better stated, as you begin to remember — this powerful Law of Attraction, the evidence of it that surrounds you will be easily apparent, for you will begin to recognize the exact correlation between what you have been*

thinking about and what is actually coming into your experience. Nothing merely shows up in your experience. You attract it — all of it. No exceptions.

Because the Law of Attraction is responding to the thoughts that you hold at all times, it is accurate to say that you are creating your own reality. Everything that you experience is attracted to you because the Law of Attraction is responding to the thoughts that you are offering. Whether you are remembering something from the past, observing something in your present, or imagining something about your future, the thought that you are focused upon in your powerful now has activated a vibration within you — and the Law of Attraction is responding to it now.

For a better understanding of this, I highly recommend the book *The Law of Attraction* by Esther and Jerry Hicks where the Teachings of Abraham are brought to life. "Abraham" (the name chosen by a group of evolved non-corporeal teachers), communicates and shares the group's broader spiritual perspective through the physical apparatus of a woman called Esther. This book goes into great detail on the Law of Attraction and how to apply it to *all* the different areas of your life.

I bring this Law and these teachings to your attention to help you understand *how* you can regain control of your life and actually create the reality you desire by using effective tools rather than constantly trying to manipulate the world outside of yourself, which I used to do for a long time without attaining the results I desired. An understanding of these principles can help you to take control of your life and work in partnership with the Universal energy that governs all things.

Your "Inner Know it All"

Another principle and concept I would like to bring to your attention is that of your invisible "Inner Know it All".

It's the voice that speaks within you. Despite what any other person tells you, or any logical argument or belief system offered up to you to follow or to sway you from or towards a certain point of view, the voice inside of you quite literally *Knows it All*.

It knows the Divine intelligence of the Universe. It knows your past, present and future. It knows what's best for your own highest good, as well as the highest good of the planet, the world, and whomever you might be interacting with in the moment.

Throughout this book I will often refer to this Inner Know it All as Your Inner Voice, Truth, Who You Really Are, Your Inner Knowing, or Your True Self.

The expansive part of the Universe dwells *within* you, speaking to you through what might seem like a voice, an inner feeling, a nudge, or a knowing without you even knowing *how* you know. It's the voice beyond the thought of reason that makes itself known in your head. It is Absolute Truth.

This Truth can be experienced through that knowing or feeling in the pit of your stomach. When you hear people say, "something just told me..." or "I just had a feeling..." or "I just knew..." it's this Inner Know It All to which they're referring. It's the genius thought that just seems to appear in your mind, as if it was communicated to you from an outside source.

What You Can Expect

In the upcoming section, you'll read more of my own stories revolving around suffering, as well as how I analyzed each scenario, questioned everything, and how my hunger to heal propelled me to seek the answers I'd never been taught. I searched for myself, but in hindsight I believe I was also searching for everyone who has ever questioned the way things are.

And now I share my insights with you.

Chapter 7:

Be Yourself Blueprint™ Explained –
Peeling Back the Layers

Through my journey of struggle and healing, I've identified seven steps, The Layers, that helped me transition from emotional pain to peace. Now I want to share those with you so you can apply them to your own individual journey. So that you may start to peel back each layer, one by one, to reveal who you really are and start living a life centered around *that* grounded person.

This isn't to say you'll need to follow the exact footsteps I took. In fact, it's quite the opposite. What I want to declare upfront is this...

Stop following in the path or footsteps of *anyone* else!

Even me.

You don't need to tramp depressingly down the safest road you were told to take. Similarly, you don't need to walk down the road that someone else has paved. The whole point of my writing this book is for you to pave a path that works best for *you*. That, in my opinion, has been the missing ingredient so many of us have been lacking in the mix of our life. Instead, from the time we exited the womb, people have been telling us who we should be and what we should do. Yeah, fuck that! Your life is yours and yours alone, and that deep sense of inner peace and fulfillment you've been craving will only come from a life you craft from the *inside-out*, based on your own yearnings and desires.

These are some key concepts and points that when implemented and practiced in *any* person's life can produces benefits. The actual positive changes will differ for every person. What I'm here to tell you is this... live your life in the way that only *you* know is best for you.

This isn't about *changing* yourself. It's about *revealing* yourself. This is about peeling back the layers, which is why I've titled each step or process as a layer because they build on one another. So, when I talk about "changing" I'm referring to changing your patterns and the faulty belief systems you've been living by that are holding you back from being, doing, and having all you desire.

I'm talking about changing the falsehoods you've collected and made your reality. I'm *not* talking about changing who you *really* are. Quite the opposite in fact. I'm talking about actually showing up as the real you. The *you* that's been dwelling inside all along, waiting for approval to come out and play in the vastness of life.

There's a *huge* difference between who you think and feel like you are in your head and heart and who you are actually *expressing* to the world.

This has been an important lesson in my own journey. I had an image in my head about who I was. About who I wanted to be. I knew what my truth was deep inside me. I could *feel* it. I could always feel it. It's the unchangeable part.

The problem was I wasn't actually *living* it. The actions I was taking, the words I was speaking, and the actual things I was doing day to day didn't accurately represent this truth. Unfortunately, when this truth is squashed, silenced and squandered, it will eat away at you from the inside out, pleading to be let out. It's a slow and painful death of Spirit. The very part that you're the most terrified to show the world is the part that, when shown, will set you free.

It's within this revelation of self where the magic happens. *That's* where life really begins.

The Layers

I'd like to briefly run through The Layers I've identified that helped me through my journey and that continue to be active forces in my life. These will be explained in greater detail in subsequent chapters where I'll also demonstrate how you can apply them practically in your own life.

Layer One is about adopting **"Mindfulness"** in everything you do. Another word for mindfulness is awareness.

It's virtually impossible to change an action or behavior that doesn't serve you without first being *aware* of what the actual behavior *is*. We can't let go of something we haven't recognized as being there in the first place!

Mindfulness helps you decipher an action or behavior that's a part of your current life, so you can ascertain whether it's of benefit or a detriment to you. It also helps you understand whether this behavior has become so second nature that you go about your life on autopilot while in actuality it's deteriorating your being.

Through examining how I was living my own life and then looking around to see how others were living theirs, I noticed how blindly many of us moved through the course of each day without noticing the effects those behaviors had on manifesting our own physical reality.

Indeed, most of us have never been taught or had these principles explained to us. Furthermore, many of us have *no idea* that we can gain control of our lives by bringing attention to our thoughts, rather than manipulating the external circumstances around us.

I intend to show you how to stop and notice not only what activities you are partaking in on a daily basis, but what thoughts you are offering up, all the way to who you're spending time with, especially in your closest circles. Believe it or not, the energies and attitudes of the people you spend the most time around can directly affect your own energy levels, thought patterns, behaviors and actions. They can also serve as an outer sign to what you are vibrating out into the world. They are reflecting back to you who you are being in the world.

Layer Two is that of **"Forgiveness."** We naturally place blame on those people who have wronged and hurt us. This can leave us in a place of feeling extremely stuck and like the only way out of the residual emotions from these hurts would be to reverse time and undo what has been done to us. While this would seem like the easiest solution, it isn't possible. And so, we must adapt tools and techniques to move forward from such hurt in a way that allows us to continue to flourish and grow while maintaining our own sense of wellbeing.

By holding on to anger and resentment towards another person, you're giving away your power to them. This only causes you pain, not the other person.

This is *not* to say that people are not victimized and that people don't do absolutely horrible things to others. They do. And I want to make very clear that forgiveness is *not* about saying what someone did was right, but rather, it's about freeing yourself from the pain and choosing to live independently from it. We absolutely cannot control other people, nor can we go back in time and stop them from hurting us, be it emotional *or* physical pain, but we can make choices for ourselves moving forward. It's *these* choices that will either set you free or keep you prisoner to your pain.

Being able to forgive a person who has wronged you is about releasing the emotions that are suppressed and repressed deep within you from the pain. It's about feeling the pain fully, so that it can leave your body. This can be difficult especially depending on the severity of what you've been through. Many people spend their entire lives not wanting to look at these trapped feelings and take on many subconscious toxic behaviors in an effort to keep these emotions at bay. It is, however, in the allowing of these emotions to surface, that you'll be set free from the pain.

A large aspect of being able to forgive others, especially those who have hurt us the most, is about reframing what they've done and seeing it in the larger context of our soul's journey and evolution. This brings us into talking about Divine Contracts between souls—agreements made between two or more souls before embarking on this physical life journey.

I believe we make certain agreements with each other to help one another learn profound lessons here on Earth. It's my belief we make these agreements before we even incarnate in bodies, and that often these lessons and teachings can come in the form of struggles and pain and even wrong doings by other people towards us.

In a broader perspective, I view these wrong doings as gifts from those people that help us integrate the different lessons our soul came here to learn. This results in our own personal growth as people, *as well* as the overall growth of our soul, which travels with us from lifetime to lifetime. This can be hard to absorb and accept, depending on how deep the wounds are that another has inflicted upon you, but this perspective has greatly helped me to release the blame towards other people in my life for why they made certain choices.

In the chapter on forgiveness, I will go into more detail on Divine Contracts and specifics to the contracts in my own life with certain people.

In order to move forward towards healing emotionally and living a life of peace and joy, it's essential that we move past these old hurts. Not only move forward from them, but also find *empowered meaning* within the pain they have caused us.

Forgiveness isn't only reserved for those people who have deeply hurt us, but also for *ourselves*, the person we can often be the toughest towards and on whom we place blame. Forgiving ourselves is just as important as forgiving other people in our lives— past and present. We'll explore this in great depth within this chapter.

Big miracles begin showing up when we forgive.

In the Forgiveness chapter I'll show you how to let go of past hurts, as well as how to make forgiveness a daily practice.

Layer Three is that of learning how to **"Follow Your Guidance."**

In Western culture we're rarely taught we have an inner guidance system, let alone given the tools on how to use it or sharpen it. We often feel alone and unsupported, yet we're born into this time-space reality with a flawless compass designed to help guide and direct us through our lifetime. This built-in compass is rarely acknowledged, let alone utilized. Not only is this guidance not encouraged, but we're also taught to fight *against* it.

We don't need to feel lost. We don't need to walk through life, feeling scared and alone when our absolute best friend and support system lies *within* us all the time. Like a muscle, with consistent use, it becomes stronger and easier to use and trust.

This is the sacred information we need to utilize. This is the energy within each and every one of us that we need to tap into in order to create a world of peace and prosperity. It's my absolute belief that one day this will be common knowledge and something we teach our young generations from the get-go in school. But for now, let's start with *you*!

Let's start by tapping you back into your own internal compass, shall we?

I've broken down this compass system into two specific sections that make it all come together as one. These two components are:

1. **Passions and Is-ness,** and

2. **Intuition**

These are not gifts that some people are lucky enough to be born with and others miss out on. Rather, they are systems that some people learn to pay close attention to and develop over time through consistent practice. You can do this too!

Some people automatically follow this guidance without naming it while others, like myself, have had to *learn* how to use it and consciously put a title to it in order to apply and exercise it. Hence, both groups of people have lives that seem to just effortlessly *flow*. Things just seem to work out for them! They are guided and most importantly, they follow through on this guidance.

It's my goal throughout this book to show you how to recognize and work with these systems, and then practice them to the point that they become natural reflexes without constant thought and analysis. For myself, knowing and utilizing these tools has allowed my loneliness to dissipate, my sense of feeling supported to heighten, and my sense of overall wellbeing to manifest.

When you become aware of the understanding that you're being guided minute to minute through what can sometimes feel like a chaotic life, you'll invariably experience a calming sense of peace. When you go out into the world from a grounded space of inner peace, then you'll experience miracles unfolding and be aware enough to *recognize* them! It also makes dealing with the inevitable challenges of life and growth easier.

After learning to follow our guidance, we will move to **Layer Four**, that being to **"Take *Inspired* Action."**

The important aspect in this layer is to take action *once* you've tuned in to your Guidance System. Action taken without guidance cannot only be non-productive, but can actually be detrimental to our emotional and physical health and wellbeing. It causes more exertion of effort than is necessary. Yet, being inspired and guided *without* taking action causes stagnation. The two complement each other.

Using our guidance to inspire action can produce *gigantic* results in our lives, yet as we grow up and reach adulthood we're taught the exact opposite. We live in a world based on a "go, go, go" mentality, which can have detrimental results on our health and wellbeing and even contribute to us literally working ourselves to death. This is the message our parents and society passed down to us from one generation to another.

Exhaustion, busyness and stress have become the hallmarks of achievement and success while relaxation and ease have been associated with being lazy!

I watched my mom end up in the hospital on the brink of death from working so much. Three jobs and constant exertion literally made her *collapse* in exhaustion. When I say she was on the brink of death, I'm not speaking metaphorically... after over a month of lying in a hospital bed with a virus that had spread throughout her entire blood stream and collapsed one of her lungs, the doctors told her they were certain she wouldn't make it. After having an intense out of body experience, she said she took one look at my brother and I, and then decided, *Not today, I can't leave yet. I still have something to live for.* She subsequently made a slow and painful recovery.

This notion of working hard beyond endurance became my model on how to be successful. This was how you needed to work in order to make money and live comfortably. I grew up believing this philosophy. Even after seeing my mom work herself into a near death, I still didn't learn. It was only when I experienced the near death of my *soul* that I began examining my own patterns of belief and behavior around success.

Plowing forward isn't the answer.

No amount of action can make up for a misalignment with your inner self—your *True* Self. Indeed, it's important to grasp the notion that you cannot compare your actions with somebody else's. Your pathway is an individual one and there's no *one* manual for all of humanity to follow. Yet, we're encouraged to follow particular pre-set pathways to success set up by those who have trod ahead of us. What we *actually* need to do is forge our own pathways that are in alignment with our individualized life purpose. In this chapter I intend to remind you how to tune in to those aspects of yourself that will guide you, and will ultimately help you take massive action *from* this inspired place.

Judgments and opinions from others, as well as your own ego, are inevitable, especially when you start shedding layers and embracing who you *really are*. Which leads me to **Layer Five—"Let Go."**

People are going to criticize you. People are going to tell you your ideas are wrong. People are going to disagree with the way you choose to live your life, the projects you're inspired to undertake, the things you say, and the actions you take.

I know... this is probably not what you thought you were going to hear in a self-development book and most certainly probably not what you *wanted* to hear!

I used to think that life was about figuring out what things I needed to do so that people wouldn't judge or criticize me. Once I knew what these "things" were *then* I could put every bit of force and energy into becoming them. Then, and *only* then, would the world like and accept me. Then I could find love, acceptance and approval in the eyes of another. What I was really craving was this love, acceptance and approval from myself.

The problem, and it's a *big* problem, is that no two people view the world exactly the same way. No two people have the exact same ideals of what makes a "perfect" world and what makes a "perfect" person.

So then, how could I become what was expected of me if the playing field and the goal posts were constantly changing, depending on who I was around and what environments I found myself in? The answer was plain and simple. I couldn't. And neither can you. It's impossible. And it shouldn't *be* possible.

For me the over-riding lesson came in understanding that one of my true life challenges was about me getting solid with myself and knowing who I was so that I would be unshakeable in a firestorm of judgments. That occurs when I'm just being myself and accepting that self. Rather than falling in line with someone else's idea of acceptable or possible in my life, I now make all my decisions based on my inner guidance system.

While letting other people's opinions go is absolutely crucial in living from your deepest center, there's one more person's opinion that must be released. This one might not be obvious. This one has a tricky way of sneaking up on you.

This one is your own opinion of *yourself...* the opinion of your ego. The thought of who and what you *should* be that runs rampant through your head and can grab hold of the steering wheel of your desires and deepest yearnings. Sometimes the most unrecognizable criticisms of all come bombarding from this part of you. And, therefore, they are the most important to release.

In this section we will also talk about letting go of life circumstances and situations. These can be difficult to let go of because we feel powerless to control them. And while this is somewhat true, we have much more power than we believe. We ultimately have the power to co-create and use the laws of the Universe to control how we react to every situation that arises.

Following on is **Layer Six,** which is that of **"Embodiment."**

While all these steps are important to implement in your daily life practices, I've presented all seven layers in a particular order for a reason. While you can gain massive benefits in your life from implementing these ideas, it's difficult to do one without ingraining the previous ones first. Therefore, it's important to take each step in sequence or peel back each layer in the order they're presented.

I've read dozens of self-help and self-growth books in an attempt to learn and educate myself, as well as to gain resources I feel the traditional school system failed to teach. And while these books and tools have been *massively* helpful in bringing me back to myself, to merely understand them on an intellectual level isn't enough. The practices must be *implemented,* so that we become the *embodiment* of that which we most admire and aspire to be.

In this section, we will look at and learn how to become living examples of that which we desire in our daily life through the actions we take and the energy we choose to vibrate, as both a state of being *and* as a verb. The learned theory thus translates from an idea into *action*.

For a long time I dabbled in meditation, comprehending its benefits and effects. Yet repeatedly I would cease actually practicing it, which is ironic because I was preaching it to others. I came to recognize that without consistent practice I couldn't possibly reap the benefits in my own life.

The same goes for health and fitness. Many of us know what foods are healthy and will provide our bodies with nutrients and fuel, giving us energy to be the best versions of ourselves. Yet we continue to be inactive and eat greasy fast food and sugar-laden desserts. If this pattern continues then nothing will change.

Embodiment. *Being* that which you *understand*.

After embodying that which we wish to have more of in our lives, we're pretty much on the road to success unless, of course, we're still following in the footsteps of somebody else who has deemed themselves to be successful or by trying to show up as someone other than ourselves which leads me to **Layer Seven —"Be Your Fucking Self!"**

Originally, I had titled this layer "Becoming You", but there was something about the phrasing that just didn't sit with me. I soon realized the reason for my discomfort was the word "becoming", and this is why... you can't *become* that which you already *are*.

It's who you are. It's your core. It's unchangeable and unbreakable. IT IS YOU!

You can't become that which you already *are,* and all of this work is really about ripping away and shedding extraneous layers that have been built up around this core, so you can shine super bright like the star you are. That's why it's our final layer!

It's all the junk we accumulate around this core that gives us a misplaced belief of who we actually are. All the ideas from our ego and the world of what we should or shouldn't be. Falsehoods. Illusions. Barriers that hold us back from being and expressing the fullest degree of our true nature.

This last step is about really owning and harnessing this truth of you and letting it shine in the world. It's one thing to *feel* like who you want to be and what you know to be true, but it's a whole different experience when you outwardly express this truth to the world and allow other people to really *see* you.

This is where the magic happens. This is the key piece. This is the most beautiful thing on Earth! And you've seen it in others.

You've seen it in the woman who's so embodied in this state of grace that she moves with utmost ease when doing something as simple as walking down the street.

You've seen it in the expressed view of the person whose opinion contradicts everyone else's in the room yet they confidently speak it regardless.

You've seen it in the person whose outfit stands out with creative splendor in a room full of corporates.

You've seen it in the people making a living, doing what everyone else thought was impossible.

You see it everywhere. Yet there is a high probability you're not *living* it. And that's okay. I spent a lot of my life not living it either. But I walked the path from that place to the place I'm in now and so can you. And, best of all, this transition can flow.

So don't beat yourself up for not being wherever you want to be yet. You are where you are and that's beautiful! Enjoy the unveiling of the person you really are. Enjoy the living *into* your deepest truth. We can't get there by skipping the journey. That's the best part, and only a teaser of what's to come.

We were all born into the world as unique individuals differing in every beautiful way, yet we grow up in a society where we're taught to stifle our own flame. To dilute who we are. To tone down our true colors. To reshape those parts of ourselves that don't fit into the box.

Together let's make a conscious choice to work outside of this default operating system the rest of the world uses. Let's live a different model. Ultimately, through speaking, acting, and embodying your truth you can fully express who you are to the world. You don't need permission from anyone to do that.

It's my hope that you honor and own your true self— the part that's completely unique and individualized to *you*. We're not all following the same generic blueprint. We're not all meant to be identical versions of each other.

The information in this book is here to help you break down these layers and come back in contact with the true unique you, so you can outwardly express yourself to the world.

Let's get started!

Chapter 8:

Layer 1 – Mindfulness

I started casually smoking when I was in junior high school at the age of fourteen. I started innocently enough with Captain Black cigars, which I smoked only on weekends with friends out at "bush parties" where we'd all gather around big bonfires in empty fields, drinking and smoking until the sun came up or our parents found us after breaking curfew, whichever came first.

I then progressed from casual cigars to casual cigarettes, and only smoked when I was intoxicated. Eventually I smoked regularly around friends—sober or not.

I don't even fully understand or remember *why* I started smoking in the first place. To be cool? To fit in? To rebel? Maybe it was a combination of all those reasons. There is one thing I can be certain of, and that's that this social form of self-abuse eventually led me to become a full-blown, cigarette smoking, nicotine *addict*.

Those little white devils became my crutch in a very serious way. I turned to them for solace and to comfort selective emotions while suppressing others. I sometimes felt they helped me to cling to and belong to a group of friends while other times, when situations became overwhelming, they offered me an escape route from a conversation I didn't want to be a part of. They were reliable. They never let me down, never failed me, and never abandoned me. Even when everyone else in the world turned against me, I knew I could turn to my little, white stick friends.

After my breakup with Keeth, my dependence on cigarettes skyrocketed to an *all* time high. Coerced with vodka, beer, and blow, they were the perfect fit for my self-created "support system." I would sit on my porch, smoking not one, not two, but sometimes three or four back to back, lighting the fresh, crisp tobacco-encased cylinder off the smelly stump of the one I'd just polished off. One after the other... any attempt to fill the heart shaped hole within me.

I don't know what exactly triggered the strong desire in me to quit, but it came a few months after the breakup that shattered me into a million little pieces. I knew I couldn't repair the relationship and I knew I couldn't repair Keeth, so I began taking little steps in the direction of *self*-repair.

Something had to give.

I experimented with the then popular e-cig which is an electronic cigarette that vapor nicotine cartridges plug into, allowing the user to still get a hit of nicotine, but without all the harmful toxins of the chemical laden tobacco. While this did help to keep me away from the real things most of the time, I felt as though I was simply upgrading my wheelchair to a walker. It was an improvement, but it was clear that I still wasn't walking on my own two feet.

It wasn't until I found Alan Carr's *Easy Way to Quit Smoking* that my lungs were able to liberate themselves from the tar-soaked toxins I had covered them in for years.

I did this through becoming present with my cigarette every time I smoked one—not allowing my phone or thoughts to distract me from the task at hand.

From a non-smoker's point of view, this would seemingly be a *simple* task, but I can assure you that it was very difficult indeed, and my mind tried desperately to distract me from focusing on the very thing that was slowly stealing both the life and energy from my body.

When we participate in an action that the bigger part of us, our Higher Self, knows to be detrimental to our health, then our ego and Lower Self will try everything to take our focus off what we're actually doing, in an effort to keep the emotions bubbling below the surface suppressed. When we see our destructive actions with clear eyes, you'd think our natural inclination would be to stop them in a bid to improve and heal ourselves. Not always true. The ego can, in fact, do the opposite by seeking to sabotage our efforts. Even simply seeing this pattern for what it really is can help us grow.

I made it my personal goal to become present with my cigarette in every moment we were intimate, tasting the filter and feeling the denseness of the smoke as it travelled from my mouth, down the passage of my throat, settling deep within the tissues of my lungs where it lingered before reversing the path out of my body.

My eyes observed the smoke as it travelled from my mouth to the air in front of me. My nose tingled as it took in every aspect of the smell, thick and musky, clogging my nostrils with every whiff. I did all I could to remain neutral in my opinions and judgments that naturally wanted to surface through this process. Over and over again I was reminded just how disgusting and gross the habit of swimming in filthy smoke was.

Every time my mind wandered to thoughts of condemnation, I returned my focus to the task at hand— the task of observation. I began noticing the physical sensations of each inhale and exhale as well as the emotional sensations of tension and anxiety that were temporarily relieved in the moment of each suspended inhale—only to return with more fierceness as my parted lips pushed the cloud out from my body.

The more I was able to observe my actions without sentencing them to a jail of self-hatred, the easier it was for me to change them. Once you come to a certain level of awareness about one specific area of your life or a particular behavior, try as you might, it's next to impossible to go back to your naivety in ignoring the damage you're causing yourself. When the ray of light shines, then the darkness cannot prevail. It would require a lot of work for it to make its presence dominant again.

With continued increased awareness around my cigarette addiction, I started to see that this "little" action had enslaved my whole life. It left me constantly worrying and planning my next escape from reality via the mechanism of the inhale and the exhale, which represented a moment of release.

I dedicated myself to continually transforming the question of "how can I eliminate this habit from my life?" to "why would I *include* this destructiveness in my life?" This shift sparked subtle transitions in my consciousness—some that I was aware of and some that were underlying.

I was determined to shift my perception from a place of desperately trying to quit smoking to a viewpoint of it seeming like a brilliant idea to quit smoking in order to gain increased health and vitality in my life. Instead of beating myself up for something I knew was terrible for me and socially frowned upon, I instead dedicated myself to awareness.

If I couldn't change my action from the outside, I knew I could change my focal point from the inside.

Surprisingly, after gaining this awareness, the action steps to actually quitting came easily and effortlessly. And this came from a person who swore up and down for almost a decade that she didn't even *want* to quit because she "enjoyed" smoking *that* much!

If I can do it, I assuredly have the faith that you can do it as well. And that doesn't just go for smoking, but for any addiction, or large or small behavior you engage in and want to change.

The Bigger Picture

It's common for most of us to unconsciously travel throughout our day, bumping along with little focus on what we're doing, where we're going, and how we're acting.

Unconscious moments strung together create an unconscious day that when strung together create a life of unconsciousness. When this happens, we begin to let our habits and routines dictate our days, how we'll behave, and what actions we'll take or not take. Thus, we allow our current circumstances and situations to shepherd us through life, whisking us through rather than having intention-focused forward movement.

In order to make *any* change, adjustment, or transformation in your life, it's first essential to observe and be aware of where you are *right NOW*. And as shitty as it can feel to look your current reality directly in the eyes, it's what's necessary to create forward momentum away from what's undesirable and towards what we actually want.

Where's the starting point?

It's similar to looking at a map. How do you know which direction to start walking or driving in if you don't even know where you currently are? The

"YOU ARE HERE" marker is absolutely essential before taking steps towards your desired destination.

Unfortunately, no one explains to us how to read and interpret our life map when we exit the womb, and so it's left up to us to analyze and observe where we are, so we can begin traveling forward.

With that, there are three key areas I've found to be essential in becoming present to determining your current reality or *starting point*:

1. **WHO** you spend your time with

2. **HOW** you spend your time

3. **WHAT** you're aware of in your body and emotions.

The Three Keys

Being aware and being mindful is enough to start you transitioning into the life you deeply desire, but to create *lasting* change with a deeper sense of ease, it's important to break down the different aspects of life around which you actually want to create mindfulness.

Analyzing *who* I was spending time with, *how* I was spending my time, and becoming aware of *what* was going on with my body, my thoughts, and my emotions were the key points in me making the transition from partying, self-sabotage, and overall self-hatred into self-acceptance, love and approval. They are aspects I continue to be mindful of as I move forward into different chapters of my life and anytime I want to make a change, but feel as though I'm coming up against something that causes me to feel stuck. These keys can be used for small, seemingly insignificant changes, as well as for bigger, life-altering changes and transitions. Here I will break down each key specifically.

WHO you spend your time with

Sometimes it's easier to gain insight into our lives by looking at the people we surround ourselves with. The people we spend time with can often show us what we need to see within ourselves... an external reflection of our internal world whether it's good, bad or neutral.

Essentially, without our relationships, we're nothing... we'd cease to exist, at least in a physical sense. We'd have no concept of who we are because we wouldn't be able to witness ourselves in relation to anything or anyone else. These people and our relationships mirror back to us what we need to see within ourselves. They indicate how we're showing up in this world, despite how we *claim* we're showing up. It's all too easy to create an image in our minds— an ideal of who we want to be and the life we want to live, but then not have our actual life match this image. This can be a powerful manifestation tool yet it can also work against us when we get stuck *living* in the image—denying what's really going on, how we're spending our time, and with whom it's being spent.

As mentioned, the people in our lives mirror back to us both the light and dark aspects of ourselves. The things that most irritate you about other people are actually aspects of your own dark or shadow self that you consistently deny. This can be difficult to process and accept.

When I get stuck in my ego, thinking and wanting to demand I'm right, I have a hard time with this one. I need to be gentle with myself, and drop into a place of seeing the broader picture to accept this reality and to understand what these relationships and the people within them are actually showing up to teach me.

How could it be that the things I despise in others are a reflection of who *I* really am? How could it be possible that the *one* quality in my boss, my best friend, or my boyfriend that drives me absolutely fucking insane, is the *exact* same quality in *me*?

Part of me wants to say, "Fuck that! It's all them and their shit!" which to some degree is true... it is partly their own shit. They're working through their own stuff and navigating through their own lives just as we all are.

The catch is—I wouldn't be able to perceive or pick up on this irritant if it wasn't a trigger for me. It would simply float on by. It's a trigger *because* I need to pay attention to it, and most importantly *heal* it. The fact is, I wouldn't even *notice* these innate qualities within someone else if there was no resonance deep within me.

What would actually *benefit* me is to thank this person silently for being there. For showing up and shining the light on the dark cobwebbed corners of myself that I wouldn't otherwise be able to decipher and thus *heal*.

An example from my own life of "looking in the mirror" has been my relationship with money. It's been a challenge throughout my life, having been raised mostly by a single mother who was always struggling to make ends meet where there were times just getting food on the table seemed difficult. Even at a young age, I picked up on this struggle our family faced, and the anxiety it caused my mom. The worry subsequently passed down to me, and the same old story continued on into my adult life. Yet, I didn't even realize it.

Instead of wanting to relive her past, as well as my childhood, I made a decision I would absolutely never live like my family had while I was growing up. Instead, I would earn money, sustain and support myself through hard work, and in the process prove myself worthy.

Sounds like an ideal woman to grow into, right? I thought so too, but now I see things much differently. I see the truth *behind* the front of working endlessly, so I'd never end up where my mom was. And it was still misery. Misery *and* a shitty relationship with money! Add to that exhaustion and a feeling of never being able to get ahead.

A couple of key people in my life brought my attention to this hang-up. An old employer proved to be one of my biggest triggers. I was vocal on many occasions that he was "money hungry," that all he cared about was the dollar in his pocket, that he was willing to sacrifice and overlook his employees' sense of happiness and wellbeing at the cost of making a couple extra bucks. I talked about how I noticed this person, sucking up and acting differently towards clients with money, and that he didn't care about the clients *or* his employees, but only cared about the income. I would get extremely passionate and upset when talking or even thinking about this! *Furious* actually.

It wasn't until I really started taking a deep look at not only my own financial situation, but my actual *relationship* with money that I really *saw* that everything that angered me about *him*, I might as well have been shouting at *myself*.

WOOOOWW... He wasn't the one who had money issues... I WAS! To be more accurate, maybe my old boss did too, but I'm sure I wouldn't have been seeing or picking up on so much of it were it not also for my own serious hang-ups in this area.

When I had this revelation, I began paying attention to my relationship with money and how I interacted with people when money was involved. I was astounded at what I noticed.

When my clients at the hair salon inquired about how much my different services cost, I always felt uneasy. I didn't even like saying out loud what I charged. While some clients were fine paying my prices, others would complain they were too much. In the later scenario, I would instantly get defensive and feel the need to justify to them *why* my prices were what they were. Explaining that I had been in the industry for X number of years, and attended X amount of classes— that my services were in demand and because of all these reasons, *that's* why I was charging what I was.

In reality, there was no need for me to justify or be defensive when talking to them about my prices. No matter what the price range for *any* service, it'll be too much for some people, just right for others, and possibly even too low for other people. This reaction I had was again—a reflection of *my* own relationship to money.

It was insecurity. A deep residing insecurity. A feeling of not being worthy enough to make the amount of money I desired to be able to live the lifestyle I wanted and fulfill the desires that burned deep within me. It was reflective of my lack of self-worth and not owning my own skills and the value I added to other people's lives. It had nothing to do with my boss. It also had nothing to do with the money or even the clients. They were merely showing me the issues I had to address within myself in order to live the life I wanted. The life I'd been *begging* to live through my desires and prayers. The life I'd been blaming everyone for withholding *from* me.

I'd *never* have spotted this pattern or identified this belief system without going through those experiences and without seeing all the things I didn't want to see and acknowledge in myself through my employer and through my clients' comments.

This is where a lot of people get stuck. They see a behavior or quality within someone else—a quality they loathe, and that just eats away at them every time they're around the person.

So what do they do? They leave the relationship. They quit the job. They move out of the city. *And then what?* They usually find themselves in the exact same situation with more or less the exact same person irritating them, just in a different body—*still there attempting to teach them the same lesson*. Then the pattern repeats itself until they acknowledge what it is within them they want to change and heal.

So, those people who seem to drive us bonkers and can make us feel like ripping out our hair are actually giving us a gift, even if they themselves don't see it as such. I try to take this perspective when someone is angering me or upsetting something within me. If nothing else, it's a more empowering perspective to take on than feeling like someone is personally trying to upset you.

The truth is, a lot of the time it's not even about changing the pattern and behavior so much as shining a light on it. When the light is switched on, the darkness dissipates and you automatically orient towards healing without exerting massive amounts of effort.

HOW you spend your time

One of my all-time favorite sayings is, "*How you spend your day is how you spend your life.*" It's so simple. It's so cliché. It makes all the sense in the world yet how many of us actually consider this while moving about our day-to-day life?

I believe there's a *huge* disconnect between how we imagine our lives to be, who we are and what we do, and what our lives *actually are*.

What do you spend your day *doing*? Look outside of work, and ask *how* do you spend your 'free' time during the evenings and weekends? *What* activities do you take part in? How do you *feel* when taking part in these activities? *Why* do you take part in these activities or behaviors? Is it your decision or someone else's? Are you going through your day by *default* or because you're *consciously choosing* it?

Answering these questions will help you determine where your "YOU ARE HERE" marker is in your life.

One thing I had to assess was my fitness... or lack thereof.

I've always had admiration for people, women especially, who are lean and fit. Yet, when I look back at how I was spending my time, I wasn't exactly exercising and eating nourishing food, which is the action required to being lean, fit, and strong.

While I *seemed* to place an apparent value on this lifestyle, my actual time was spent working all day and then coming home to make a big dinner before sitting down on the couch to watch TV or a movie. These behaviors didn't exactly align with being fit and healthy. Still, I felt a deep value in it and longed to be living this way.

As soon as Saturday evening rolled around and my work week came to an end, the partying began—predrinking and club hopping. Where should we all meet up to slam back a few before heading out? What bar did we want to start at? Who did we know that was working so we could skip the line? Who were we calling to score some blow? Where could we meet them? Would they drop it off if we paid extra?

A lot of the time, I barely remember much besides getting to the bar and drowning myself in booze. I would wake up the next day feeling like I'd been hit by a truck. Most of my Sundays were spent lying lifelessly on the couch, hung over as all hell, drifting in and out of sleep, and only getting up to eat or vomit. Then I'd crawl back to the couch again.

Besides the obvious physical discomfort, Sundays were always an emotional battle for me. I would fight the insidious creep in of depression, anxiety and guilt from the previous night out and the poor choices I'd made—choices I *knew* weren't in alignment with the person I wanted to be and the life I longed to be living.

It was like I put on a mask in the evening. I'd become this fun, lively and life-loving person, only to loathe myself and bathe in self regret the next day. While I didn't feel happy on the inside, I did take on that persona because deep down it's who I longed to be. I never felt good about who I was—as if there was something *wrong* with me. I felt like I had to be who I was *supposed* to be, based on all the influences of society, rather than just being myself.

Interestingly enough I had a whole network of people who spent their time doing exactly the same thing. It became normal. This was how my friends and I had fun. I had a difficult time understanding how people spent their weekend *not* hung over and hating their lives. What do you mean, you don't drink on the weekends? Committing to any activity on a Sunday wasn't even an option for me, and I found myself being shocked if someone even suggested it. Sunday was always specifically designated to nurse myself out of a hangover, and then the week was spent preparing for the following weekend to do it all over again!

This was how I spent my time. Yet, deep within, I envied people who had *real* passions. There were things I was interested in that I enjoyed doing like yoga, dancing, spending time outdoors, writing, reading, and a deep interest in physical, emotional and spiritual health. But when I actually stopped and examined my life, I saw I was literally spending *none* of my time on *any* given day doing these things.

How could I live a rich and wonderful life when I spent my time doing everything *but* the things I claimed to love doing?

It can be difficult to make changes when you partici-pate in activities that don't align with who you really are and want to be, and where the only people you surround yourself with are those who partake in the same destructive behaviors you do.

WHAT you're aware of in your body and emotions

Your body. Your physical flesh, blood and bones body. Oh this beautiful vehicle so often overlooked and overworked into a state of exhaustion. Ignored, abandoned, and pushed through all the tasks and jobs we assign to it every day.

When's the last time you actually tuned in and asked *your body* what it needed? How *it's* feeling?

We're conditioned to use our minds and to push past the limitations of the body. This can be an amazing quality, helping us to transcend set points of our previous behaviors or conditioning. But it can also be detrimental to our wellbeing.

When I walked away from the alcohol and drugs, as well as the entire lifestyle that came with it, I embraced a new way of living. The gym became my everything. Pushing my body through exercise to the ultimate limit of what *I knew* to be possible. I started paying attention to what I was eating and how I was fueling my body. I started calculating, measuring, and micro-managing every single morsel of food that passed my lips. I was convinced this was the answer to why I'd hated every inch of my body for so many years. These were the tools I'd been missing. Or so I thought...

What happens when your self-care practices become the ultimate and most detrimental form of self-sabotage? What happens when you cling desperately to one way of living, acting, and being in the world that it takes precedence over everything around you? When your social life is swapped for the eye contact or a mere glance or a smile and a nod you exchange with the regulars at your local gym? When meet-ups with friends become scheduled around your weekly cheat meal? Or where you stuff your face to the brink of vomiting, barely listening to what your friend is saying because you're more focused on how much food you can fit into your mouth during this one small window of enjoyment until the following week?

I'll tell you what happens... sadness and pain. A pain so deep beyond the physical it's difficult to find tangible words to attribute to it. A deep ache within the soul. A gentle voice inside, screaming to be let out, only to be stifled with planning future workouts and meals.

My entire life started to revolve around this obsession with the physical. I no longer fit in with the social groups I'd known for a long time. I didn't *belong* there anymore, although I still felt a deep need to belong *somewhere*. A need to find a new way of living that led me to adapting this lifestyle and pushing it beyond what's healthy.

I was miserable. I was tired. My body hurt. I still hated the way I looked and the way I felt. I couldn't calm my mind. And most deeply, I couldn't understand why I felt so horrible after adapting a lifestyle that everyone was telling me was healthy. I had an internal tug-of-war going on, and a voice within me *begging* me to slow down, to pay attention, while my stubborn brain and the voices from the outside world told me to keep going, to push harder and to force my way to my body goals when I honestly didn't even know what they *were*. I think *loving* my body was my ultimate goal, but that was clouded and lost in the fight to get fit.

As I started to heal from my relationship with Keeth and get out into the dating world again, I met a man who I thought would be my next serious relationship. However, within a matter of six months I destroyed this relationship in a trade-off for the lifestyle to which I was clinging. I was in control, never allowing myself to surrender to life nor to this gentle man who wanted to cherish me. I pushed him away to the point of no return. He walked away with little more than a goodbye and never looked back.

Here I had been, thinking I was being the "perfect girlfriend" by becoming all the physical qualities I thought a man looked for in a woman, yet I had *still* managed to scare him away. Or so, this was how I felt.

I was left feeling raw, naked and vulnerable. While my lower self wanted to look at him and point out every-thing that he had done wrong, making the apparent failing of this short-lived relationship his fault, by now I knew better. I started to examine my role in the dismantling of our union and to take responsibility for the choices I'd made.

I hadn't paid attention to how I felt physically and emotionally. I chose to completely ignore how I felt in pursuit of an imagined lifestyle that dangled the golden carrot of perfection just out of arm's reach. I shut off my inner knowing to follow the exercise and diet plan handed to me, and in the process ignored my body and intuition.

While initially I blamed myself and my actions for why this man couldn't love me, over time I saw it as the Divine lesson that it was and understood that him coming into my life for the short amount of time that he did was absolute perfection. Our interaction gave me the awareness to pay attention to myself—my body, emotions, and thoughts. It also gave me the beautiful gift of really understanding that what's meant for me in this life *cannot* miss me. That the man who's meant to love me, for whatever period of time that might be, won't just walk away while I cling to the hope of something more. I'm thankful that he came into my life to give me this gift of awareness and also the gift of learning to surrender and not hold on so tightly—in essence, trusting the Universe's plan for my life, love, and relationships.

You're the only expert when it comes to accessing your inner truth, voice, and knowing.

To accomplish that you need to *feel* for the answers. This was something I had to learn how to do on my own in order to honor how I felt at any given moment, as well as help me choose exercise and food to respect and serve my body rather than force it into submission while also allowing my plan to change and be flexible day-to-day based on my needs on any given day.

When I started dating this man, I felt an inner nudge to "lighten up" so to speak on the exercise and strict meal planning to make room for the relationship and love I so deeply desired. Yet, I ignored this call from both my body and my inner truth in pursuit of what I thought I had to do to be healthy.

The fact is, health has a different meaning to every person and lifestyle. There's absolutely no one-size-fits-all way of living healthfully, or even towards attaining a lean and fit body. And even with all the experts and gurus in the fitness community, no one can possibly know the inner wisdom of your body the way you do. They don't have access to the level of information intuitively stored in your body. It's great to have these experts as guides to teach us the facts and educate us on nutrition, health and exercise, but it's just as important to *listen to your own body*.

It's impossible to tune in when you're running on high speed and zipping through life in a desperate pursuit to reach some imagined end point. Tuning in means ignoring what the outside world would have you believe and allowing your body to tell you what it needs moment to moment. And don't think for a second that every cell within you doesn't carry this knowledge and isn't willing to share it with you. In fact, these cells have been offering it up the entire time and still continue to do so now. Our response has been to shut down that natural flow of communication by a noisy chattering brain that thinks it knows best and all the external information and messages we're bombarded with—oftentimes messages that conflict with each other *and* our internal wisdom.

This wisdom can't be heard when our minds are running at full speed into the future or hanging out in the past. This wisdom can only be heard and understood when we slow the fuck *down* and just "be" in the present moment we're standing in. Only *then* can this beautiful knowing burst forth. It takes you dropping every preconceived notion of who you think you should be and how you *think* you should be conducting your life to really *hear* this and follow through with the guidance.

Listen to your body. Pay attention to how it *feels.*

Listen to how it feels when you eat certain foods. To what foods you're actually drawn to in the grocery store not by an insistent craving or a voice that says you can't, but by what the cells in your body are telling you they need for nourishment. And trust me, they'll tell you. They're trying to tell you. Stop and be mindful of them.

There are a few different ways our bodies communicate with us, and it will vary from person to person, because you're your own unique make-up of cells and energy. For me, I understand messages to make healthier decisions for my body through internal "nudges" so to speak. I've had incessant thoughts to eliminate dairy, sugar, and caffeine from my diet at different stages of my life. Rather than ignoring these prods, I pay attention and do my best to honor and follow their guidance, even when it's not necessarily something I *want* to do. It's also important to understand that what your body needs might change over time, and to give yourself permission to ebb and flow with the ever-changing messages or signals you're receiving.

Another amazingly simple way our body communicates to us is through how it feels when we eat or ingest certain foods or substances. This might seem like a difficult thing to pay attention to, but I assure you that if you just focus on being aware how your body feels, it'll become more obvious. We've just probably never been taught to turn our focus onto this part of ourselves, but rather to eat what society tells us is healthy or not.

How does your body want to move? Does it want to run through the wooded trails with a breeze blowing in your hair? Or does it want to flow and stretch yogic styles through downward dog? Does it want to lie and rest peacefully in shivassana or rejuvenate itself in bed for an extra hour? Does it want to dance, sing, and play, grooving from side to side? Does it want to be pushed and challenged through crossfit or weight lifting?

There's no programed regimen that can substitute for this kind of connection to your body. There's no workout program or food calculating that can make you happy and allow you to tune in enough to make the best decisions for your body's happiness from moment to moment. This is the kind of knowledge and wisdom the weight loss and fitness industry doesn't want you to know because once you do, the gimmicks and schemes they offer would cease to exist. The diet ads and messages would lose their effectiveness because you'd ultimately know what's best for your body, and whenever you start to waiver from this natural equilibrium, you'll feel discord.

So stop, slow down, and tune back in. Pay attention to how your body feels and what food and movement you're drawn to that make you feel vital.

That's not to say there aren't amazing professionals in the fitness and health industry that can teach you some super valuable things about your body and how it moves, as well as to offer knowledge about food and movement. I've had some wicked awesome trainers!

But I do believe their expertise should *only* be used in conjunction with your own internal awareness.

I encourage you to stay away from the TV, phone, or computer while you're enjoying your next meal and indeed all meals after for that matter. The Facebook newsfeed isn't going anywhere. The episode can be recorded. Your friends probably aren't waiting or holding their breath in desperate anticipation of what photo you'll upload next. It can wait. It can *all* wait.

Pay attention.

Be mindful.

Spiritual Bypass – Don't Deny Your Humanity

We all have a shadow self that feels irritability, hate, rage, sadness, anxiety, and many other emotions. These are aspects of you, but they are not *who* you are. They don't define you as a person or a whole being.

Sometimes this is where we can often get *stuck* in our thinking and instead of *allowing* these "negative" emotions to be felt, we hide them away. Sweep them under the rug. Pretend they aren't there.

Along my spiritual and self-growth journey, I've heard this referred to as a Spiritual Bypass. Denying your humanity. It's destructive and it's detrimental to your health. It's in the denying of these completely *normal* human emotions, that they actually become magnified.

Society has made it socially unacceptable to experience and exhibit these emotions. They are something that must be felt and dealt with alone and in silence in accordance to what we're taught. It's not proper to express intense emotions outwardly.

This approach is killing us slowly and painfully! When these feelings and emotions are denied, they only grow bigger as our inner self struggles to recognize all aspects of our being.

It's not the act of acknowledging our shadow self that allows it to grows bigger—quite the contrary actually. What you resist persists. By recognizing these less than desirable aspects about yourself, you actually take power *away* from them.

The idea is to move away from blaming others and victimizing yourself to allowing these people to be your mirrors. And from there, outing the feeling, emotion, behavior, or belief system to transform and transmute it. To feel it fully, so it can dissipate. That's the goal. That's the system of coming face-to-face with your own hang-ups.

When dating Keeth, I found myself constantly irritated by the victim mentality he displayed. He used drugs and alcohol as a way to escape his current life and reality. He would have a bad day at work and then go out for a drink (which always turned into many drinks), saying he was stressed and needed to let go and relax a little.

This drove me *crazy*! How did turning to a mind-altering substance act as a reward or release to a stressful day?

I would stifle my anger and upset about it by making subtle, yet passive aggressive comments to him like, "Well, I don't see how having a *drink* is a healthy way to deal with your problems," or "Drinking isn't a healthy way to relax," while inside I wanted to *scream*.

I was devastated when we broke up. And what did I do? I went out all weekend, getting wasted at the bar and doing blow. How *hypocritical* was that?

The very thing I hated and wanted to change about him *so* badly was the exact place I defaulted to when I was super emotional and under extreme stress. The way he dealt with his stress was one of the biggest factors leading to the end of our relationship yet I dealt with the pain of losing him in the *exact* same way.

I desperately wanted to change and correct my behavior that was mirrored back through his actions, and I was given the opportunity to heal through the ending of our relationship.

While there may be qualities in others that irritate you, often they are reflections of your own internal world. The same is also true for the qualities you *love*, *admire*, *look up to* and *envy* within another.

What impresses you about other people? What quality in another person makes you say, "Wow, I wish I was like that!" or "Wow, I wish I could do that, be that..." etc.

Well... guess what?

You can and *you are*!

Whaaat... ?

I know right! Yup, you can be the happiest and wealthiest and most successful of them all! You can be the most fulfilled, the most enlightened, and the most blissful. You can have it all! You *are* it all.

Do you ever try to help another realize their own potential and literally draw it right out of them? This is such a common way of seeing your own potential and value in the eyes of another. And when it's not fully harnessed and expressed, it can also be your greatest resistance to *fulfilling* your greatest potential. By looking at another and trying to pull the goodness out of them, you, in fact, subconsciously want to express the potential that dwells within your very being.

Keeth was an exceptionally talented tattoo artist and musician, and watching him choose to lose himself in drugs and alcohol seemed like such a waste of a precious life to me. Indeed, from my world viewpoint at the time, it felt as though I was witnessing him discard rare innate gifts that most people on Earth are neither born with nor could ever hope to develop. It was as if he had just been *given* them when he came here onto Earth while others simply weren't.

I was envious. I was envious he was so naturally gifted while I had to work extremely hard and dedicate myself intensely to anything I wanted to succeed at during my life.

I had a vision for him... a dream that he would get off the drugs, come out on the other side as a complete inspiration for others, teach and coach them through their pain, and help them to come back to themselves just as he had. I attempted to convince him of this and direct his life down this path— always telling him how many lives he could change just by sharing his life story. Just by being himself. But it wasn't to be.

Exactly two years and three months after Keeth and I broke up, I received a phone call. I'll never forget it. It's etched in my brain, my memory, my heart and every cell of my body. The call I never wanted to get. The call that *nobody ever* wants to get.

I was at work. I was standing in the staff lunch room and I hit the floor. Hard.

Keeth was dead.

He hadn't made it. He hadn't beaten the drugs and the alcohol. They had beaten him. And my life was never going to be the same because of it.

Keeth didn't get to become clean and help others. He didn't get to experience the bliss and deep fulfilled happiness that we all deserve... that is our birthright.

I can never be sure what his purpose here on Earth was during this lifetime. Only he and God can know that. But I do know what his purpose in *my* life was and the beautiful unfolding I've experienced as a result of our relationship. He helped lead me back to myself. And for that, he will *always* live on in my heart. I know he is still with me, right now, helping me tell this story and teach from it.

I love him for inadvertently showing me who I really am, and for helping me *remember* my full potential. That's the single biggest and most precious gift any human can give another.

It was only after two years of sobriety and continued, positive forward momentum in my life that I understood the dream and vision I had wasn't Keeth's at all. It was mine. It was the aspirations I had for my own life. My entire life had been leaning into it and moving towards it. Today, I'm happy to say, I'm living it.

There was a time when I genuinely thought I had been sent into Keeth's experience to help him heal.

I felt as though I'd been magically guided to him so I could, in turn, be the one who helped him recognize the light within himself. I believed we'd be together for years and years, and that, in time, he would thank me for sticking by him and for helping him live out his greatness.

It's only now that I see the opposite was true. He showed up in my life to mirror back into my eyes all the things I deeply wanted to change and heal about myself. Had he not been that push, I'd still be bumping along with a complete lack of self-awareness and blaming everyone else for not loving me, and taking zero responsibility for my own life's direction. His absence of love and approval in reality demonstrated how much I loathed and disapproved of myself. He was my reflection in every way.

You see, it's not that someone *gives* us love and then we *feel* loved, which is what I was seeking in Keeth. It's quite the opposite actually. It's only when we can show love towards *ourselves* that people will reflect this love back to us.

Mindfulness As a Way of Living

The idea of mindfulness isn't something I just want you to apply to one isolated area of your life like eating or smoking. *Mindfulness is a way of living*. It's a way of showing up and being present in the world. It's a quality to cultivate in everything you do, everywhere you go, and everyone with whom you interact. It's something that takes continual practice and conscious effort to implement.

I have notes all over my home, reminding me to be present in the moment and encouraging me to slow down and pay attention to what's directly in front of me. I think we live in a world that pushes us to exist ten steps ahead of where we actually are in time, thinking and planning followed by more thinking and planning.

As I go about my day wanting to be as time-efficient as possible while also experiencing as much joy in the moment as I can, I often stop to ask myself questions. Rather than "What's next?" I inquire, "What's now?" I comprehend that the "What's next?" is completely ineffective when I have zero awareness of what's happening now.

Whenever people used to talk to me about being in the present moment, I always wanted to shout, "What the fuck does that *mean* anyways?" Well, I now have that definition and it's in the asking of "What's now? What's right here in front of me in this very moment in time? And *how can I enjoy it*?" That's what living in the present means to me. Giving your full attention to what you're currently doing. It really *is* that simple.

Simple, however, doesn't always mean that something is easy, especially after a lifetime of conditioning to "figuring out" what's ahead of us in the future. This is what we've been led to believe would serve us best. While I assure you that having goals and intentions creates a pathway to fulfilling your destiny, without experiencing being right here right now in the moment the end goal will never quite feel like enough.

So with all that being said, I invite you to hang out where you are, right in this very moment. To observe it. To check out your "YOU ARE HERE" signage without judgment and without criticism.

Self Reflection Exercises

Ask these questions of yourself and record your answers in a journal:

- How do the people closest to you treat you? (family, friends, partner, work colleagues, etc.)

- Do any of these people belittle or manipulate you?

- Or do they light you up and encourage you to be the best version of yourself while displaying the best version of *themselves*?

- How do they interact with others?

- What is it about their interactions with you and others that irritate you, and what is it about their interactions that you most admire?

- Are you able to analyze and see where the things that irritate you about them might be the same aspects about your *own* self that irritate you?

- Conversely, are you able to analyze the qualities you most admire and look up to that might also be unexpressed qualities within yourself that are begging to be expressed?

- Can you see that how these people treat you might be a reflection of how you treat yourself and your own sense of self-worth?

Chapter 9:

Layer 2 – Forgiveness

Mark Twain once said, *"Forgiveness is the fragrance that the violet sheds on the heel that has crushed it."*

It's always, without exception, the person who's most difficult for us to forgive that we will *benefit* the most by forgiving—that by forgiving, will set us *free* and heal our heart. This is the person who has cut us the deepest and ripped the widest hole in our heart. This process of forgiveness facilitates our own healing.

Traditionally, forgiveness has been seen as someone else doing something *wrong* or *bad*, some sort of screw up, and then they're forgiven for the apparent screw up—it's excused. They are still seen as having messed up and done something wrong, but the people forgiving

141

them choose to "let it go" so to speak. To me, this type of forgiveness is still laden with undertones of guilt and shame—someone's still made to feel *wrong* even though they've been excused for their wrongdoing. It doesn't necessarily *release* the deep feelings of resentment or anger being felt towards someone.

Forgiveness in the context of self-approval, and the Be Yourself Blueprint™ acknowledges that while you DON'T condone the hurtful action inflicted on you, you CAN set yourself free by letting go of its power to keep you perpetually trapped in the whirlwind of negative feelings and emotions that accompany it. You can begin to *reframe* the "wrong" done towards you by another and start to see it as part of a perfect lesson that you were meant to learn here on Earth. Oftentimes these Divine lessons are part of our bigger life's purpose on our soul's journey. This can be extremely difficult to perceive as such, especially when you're in the middle of a painful situation. It *is* possible though. It is...

Here I share with you a personal story of forgiveness...

As mentioned previously, Keeth and I lived next door to each other both before and after we dated. Before was easy and enjoyable. After was a living hell!

After breaking up we remained in this living arrangement for nine months before I moved in with my brother who lived twenty minutes away. Those nine months were fucking torture! Every minute of them challenged my sanity, as well as my ability to put one foot in front of the other each day.

Being door-to-door neighbors, our bedroom windows almost lined up with one another. There were summer nights where I would close all my windows and smother my ears with pillows to stop from hearing the women he had over at his house. Sometimes I thought I could catch the sounds of their giggling laughter, and there were other times late at night, I swear I could hear them moan his name in fits of sexual pleasure. I'll never know if this was really what I was hearing or if it was simply my mind driving me mad. This would go on night after night. They would park their cars outside his house and sometimes even directly outside of my house. Every morning I woke up praying it had all been a bad dream, and every night I went to bed sick to my stomach—every cell in my body contracting with pain.

In the last few months of our relationship, we'd barely had sex, partly because one of the side effects of Oxy for men is temporary impotency, but *mostly* because our relationship had taken on a rescuer/victim type of role-play. He... the victim, and I... the rescuer, trying to save him from his self-sabotaging behaviors and physical addictions. Naturally, in this type of dynamic between two people the romantic and sexual passion has a way of disappearing. While I could intellectualize and *know* this is what had caused the lack of sex, I took it as a personal failure—beating myself up emotionally and not feeling good enough, sexy enough, or desirable enough. I felt I had failed him as a woman and girlfriend. I felt I couldn't give him what he needed or wanted and, because of that, he was finding it elsewhere.

During this relationship, and pretty much every other romantic relationship I'd ever been in, my biggest fear was not being able to provide my man with what he wanted from me. In other words, not being able to keep him happy and fulfilled sexually. Instead, I shut down. I felt as though I had failed at what I feared failing the most. When Keeth made love to all those anonymous women I began facing the ultimate form of rejection over and over again. I thought they were filling the void that I wasn't able to. I believed they had something I didn't, and that they could provide for him what I couldn't. It shattered and crushed me on an incredibly deep level.

I felt rejected by the man I loved—the man I wanted more than anything to love and cherish me. All my fears came up and struck me directly in the face like bricks—each one knocking me further to the ground.

I hated him for his selfishness, and also because of his ability to just walk away and forget about me, replacing my spot in his bed with random women every night. I'd bought him those fucking sheets! I felt as though I'd been thrown away for something or someone better...

as if I was a useless piece of trash tossed onto the side of the road.

I hated myself for failing to be the partner I wanted to be—that I so deeply desired to be. Not sure how to articulate or deal with the pain I was feeling, I internalized it.

The day finally came where it was time for me to move out and move on. Our lease was finally up, and my housemates and I dispersed. It was a bittersweet day. My roommates and I moved our respective belongings out of the house. We cleaned the space so it was spotless. The carpet cleaners came in to do their job, and when the house was empty, I went back to lock up for the last time.

I sat on the kitchen counter, looking around and reflecting on the last two years of my life that had been spent there. I relived the moments of pleasure, laughter and joy, as well as the moments of tears and breakdowns. I didn't know where in that vast array of emotions I could even draw breath. But what I did know is that I was saying goodbye to a long and drawn out chapter in my life. A chapter I wanted desperately to be finished while at the same time wanting to keep writing. I didn't have a choice anymore. This was the way life had directed me and it was away from here.

I suddenly realized I'd prolonged this day for far too long, and that I'd been clinging and maintaining my connection to him by remaining in this place. I hadn't really let go. Wanting something more. Even though we weren't together, I knew he was there... just a door or a wall away. I knew that even if I couldn't talk to him directly that I could still see him if I really wanted or needed to. Living next door to him still gave me an "in" to his life even if he refused to have me be a part of it. Living with my roommate, his sister, kept me connected to him in an obscure and roundabout way. Moving away was going to sever this connection once and for all.

There was one thing I still had to do to get closure, and that was to say one last goodbye to him. I ran outside to my car, rummaged through it, and found a pen and piece of paper, as well as a random envelope. I went back into the house and wrote him a note. It wasn't long and drawn out. It said what I needed to say and what I wanted him to know.

> *Keeth,*
>
> *I just wanted to write you and tell you that I forgive you for everything. Through our relation-ship and the ending of it, I've learned so much about myself and I want to thank you for your role in that.*
>
> *I wish the absolute best for you moving forward.*
>
> *I will always love you.*
> *Katherine*

I reread the note, took a deep breath, slid it into the envelope and sealed it shut. On the front in large capital letters I wrote, "KEETH."

I said a final goodbye to the house and walked next door to his house where his brother Eric and his band mates were unloading equipment from their trailer from their previous night's show. His brother told me Keeth was home, but still sleeping. I don't know if I felt disappointed or relieved.

I extended my shaking hand clasped around the envelope, and asked Eric to *please* make sure Keeth got it. I felt his penetrating gaze and then he replied, "Of course I will, Kat, of course I will."

My eyes welled up. I walked into Eric's arms without making eye contact with him. I gave him a big hug before turning and practically running towards my car where I knew I could privately release all the pent up emotion bubbling inside of me.

I closed the door, backed out of the driveway, and drove away. The two houses grew smaller and smaller in my rear view mirror, as I repeated my prayer of forgiveness towards Keeth. I was ready to let him and this part of my life go for no other reason than I knew I *had* to.

I drove around the corner and lost sight of the houses and never went back...

Until… Eighteen months later, only days after Keeth's passing, I returned.

I pulled up to see a giant blue metal storage pod plonked on the driveway, being filled with Keeth's belongings. He didn't need them anymore. I stopped the car and nervously walked into the house, knowing he wouldn't be there but wanting nothing more than to see his face again, embrace him, look into his eyes and ask him if he had read my letter.

Walking into his bedroom was like walking into my past. I knew the empty hope-filled dream I had held onto for so long could *never* be fulfilled. Then every moment we shared together flashed through my mind like a film—every scream, every angry word, every kiss, every love scene, and every whisper of, "I love you, hunny," danced through the air. Then they were gone. Only the fragments of his life remained scattered across his bedroom floor.

I had come to help his family clean out his house. In doing so I could heal my own grief. As I shuffled through a stack of papers and mail stored in the shelves alongside his bed, deciphering what was important to keep and what seemed like trash, I came across it. The envelope. The envelope with my unmistakable writing scrolled across the front. The envelope I had handed to Eric less than a year and a half prior.

Unopened.

I hit the floor in a sack of tears and a pile of sadness.

He hadn't read it.

He hadn't even *opened* it.

The very last conversation we had together flashed through my mind. It was five months prior at his sister's wedding. I was a bridesmaid.

The wedding was at a hall in the country. Everyone had driven there to spend the night in their campers, trailers, and tents. It was late and I was exhausted from the long day. I walked outside through the double doors of the hall, only to encounter Keeth, having a smoke with a mutual buddy of ours.

The buddy excused himself—possibly sensing a private conversation needed to take place.

I walked directly up to Keeth to say hello, and he said to me, "I know you probably hate me, and you should."

To which I replied, "Keeth, I don't hate you and I never have. My life has changed so much since we were together."

The note I had written flashed through my mind. I asked myself, *Doesn't he know I don't hate him?* I had so clearly stated in my letter that I forgave and loved him.

"I know," he answered, "I see how well you're doing and all the things you're accomplishing and that's why

I had to let you go, Katherine. I was destroying you. I was taking you down with me. I couldn't keep doing that, so I pushed you away from me."

"But I'm doing good now," he continued, "I've really changed and I'm doing really good, Katherine."

A part of me knew this wasn't true, but a bigger, deeper part of me wanted to believe it was.

"I'm glad, Keeth. That makes me so happy to hear and I'm really glad for you."

With that we gave each other a deep hug and said goodnight. I retired to my trailer for bed and he went inside to the party.

I didn't see him the following morning. What I didn't know was that the hug we shared the night before would be our last. That the brief conversation we had would also be our last. I didn't know that the next time I would see Keeth would be with his hands draped gracefully across his chest, eyes closed, skin pale, and legs disappearing underneath the lid of the casket. I also didn't know my last kiss to him would be my warm lips planting on his cold, lifeless cheek in a final goodbye.

I don't think I would have been able to deal with Keeth's death had I not truly and deeply forgiven him and forgiven myself for the path our relationship had taken and the ending of it. This knowledge gave my mind a fragment of peace to hold onto in the midst of pure unadulterated agony. In the time between the ending of Keeth's and my relationship and his death, I got really honest with myself about my own emotions. The sadness, resentment, and pain. I felt them fully and I forgave them, him, and myself. It was through these three aspects that I was able to heal and transform.

The Three Aspects to Forgiveness

Forgiveness does not mean you excuse a person's behavior or even your own behavior, rather, that you choose to release it and no longer allow it or the perpetrator to have power over you. It's a means of freeing you from that which seems unfreeable. It's a way of allowing yourself to continue living the life you deeply desire despite the things that have happened or been said to you and when others have seemingly wronged you.

As the Buddha describes it, holding a grudge or not forgiving someone is like drinking poison and expecting the other person to die. Holding blame and resentment towards another person holds you in a place of disallowing your own natural flow of wellbeing. It thwarts your progress and movement forward in life while doing absolutely nothing to the person to whom you are holding the grudge.

This bitterness and resentment gets trapped in not only our emotional self but in our physical cells as well, creating disease in our bodies and debilitating our minds.

There are three major aspects to forgiveness that are absolutely vital to our wellbeing. They give us the ability to move forward in our lives with a sense of freedom and bliss. These areas are:

1. **Forgiving others**

2. **Forgiving yourself,** and

3. **Forgiving life situations and circumstances.**

When you venture down any of these three avenues of forgiveness they will produce uplifting benefits for you and propel you along the path of your own healing, but when combined *together* with equal focus and intention, that's when you truly are set free from resentment and stuckness.

I want to more specifically talk about and break down each aspect of forgiveness.

Forgiving others

It's nearly impossible to forgive anyone, including yourself, with the conditioned mentality you've acquired through life. This subconscious belief system has been ingrained and reiterated to us from childhood into our adult lives. It goes something like this:

People have done us wrong.

Everyone around us needs to act a certain way.

People are either good or bad.

Things are either right or wrong.

And all of this is etched in a black and white way of acting in this world.

This way of thinking has probably caused you many grievances up until now and will most certainly continue to do so unless you make a different choice, and that's to reframe and examine other people's actions, including your own, in a way that's different than you have up until now. This worldview then becomes empowering rather than disempowering.

What if we're *all* just doing the best we know how to do? What if the choices we make and the actions we take are the best ones we know how to from the place we're standing in our lives at any one moment? What if *no* act in the entire world was perpetuated out of hatred and only from a place of love? Could this be so? Could it?

No act is out of hate. Every act is out of love.

You're probably thinking... *What. The. Fuck. There's no way!*

How then would you explain people cheating, lying, stealing, and killing? You call that an act of love?

Yes.

Yes, I do.

Or rather... I've chosen to reframe these hurtful painful acts. I've chosen to look at this from a perspective of people attempting to love *themselves*. What if every selfish and unloving choice made or action taken was really the person's attempt to show *themselves* love? What if they just got mixed up along the way?

Would it make it easier to forgive a person with the understanding or attempted understanding that they only did what they did or said what they said because they were trying to meet their own need for love?

Maybe this is difficult for you to comprehend. But I can tell you one thing... it's a viewpoint that makes it easier to forgive another for something that feels awful. And another thing I know for certain is that I don't want to live my life holding onto resentments and grudges. Because of this, I choose to see the world and myself through this perspective. I also choose to adopt the idea that every one of us is making the decisions we think in the moment are the best for us at the time we make them.

Could it be any other way?

I don't believe any person would make a conscious decision to sabotage themselves or another—it's *always* an attempt to have a need met. Always. Even when it comes across as being totally screwy.

It has greatly helped me to understand why the people in my life have made the choices they have—many of which have caused me pain and anguish. This has allowed me to move from a place of condemnation and blame to a place of understanding and compassion. At the very least it gets me to a place of beginning to attempt to understand why people have made the choices they have and allowed me to move forward from beating my head against a brick wall in the pursuit of an answer to "why" and all the way through to understand that they really are just doing the best they know how from where they're standing. And really, that's all I can ask of someone and even *myself*.

It's helped me to understand my own life choices, as well as the actions I took and the spiteful words I've used, which I later deeply regretted. As a result, I've been able to be gentle towards myself and use forgiveness as a tool to create happiness and emotional freedom even when I don't do or say the *right* thing.

Forgiving yourself

It's been my experience that it's all too "easy" and "simple" to forgive and move forward from the pain that has been inflicted by another, only to internalize those feelings by turning inward to blame ourselves. This was my experience in the ending of my relationship with Keeth. I went through a lot of internal work forgiving him over and over again for the pain he seemingly "put" me through only to turn around and blame myself for how things ended up—for teaching him how to treat me and for allowing the relationship to take the course it did. I hated myself for not being able to help him, for not being able to articulate what my terms of a relationship meant, and for feeling like I completely failed him as a sexual partner.

After doing the "work" of forgiving him, I went down a dark and bothersome road of beating myself up for getting involved in such a relationship. I went from blaming him to blaming myself. I knew who he was and his behaviors long before we entered our relationship. I knew his life often revolved around the attention of women stroking both his ego and his dick. Heck, I was one of those girls. I was just persistent enough until I was awarded the title of "girlfriend." I allowed myself, and on some level, *wanted* to get swept into the hurricane of his life, to be the center of his attention, and to blush at every flattering compliment he gave me, which would invariably have me panting and begging for more.

I knew he thrived on the rock star persona he had created for himself. All the club managers knew him by name, lots of people looked up to him as an artist and musician, and others were completely jealous of his creative accomplishments. I knew about his addictive behaviors with drugs and alcohol from the beginning. I excused them in our relationship because my mind was clouded by love and lust. I rationalized his situation—after all, every legendary musician had demons didn't they? To be honest, there was a part of me that secretly admired all these qualities even though down the road I resented them and used them against him.

In getting into this relationship, I wanted to fit a certain image. I wanted people to see me in a certain way. I wanted people to look at me, as well as the relationship I was in, and feel admiration. I think on some twisted level, I even wanted them to be jealous of the fact that I got to be with Keeth. I got off on this attention. It made me feel significant. I was more concerned with what complete strangers thought about my relationship than I was with how I actually *felt within my relationship.*

The irony was that lots of people DID notice my relationship, but for the exact opposite reasons I wanted. I had an illusion I was in control of my life and how people perceived me, and it proved to be just that... an *illusion.*

So even though I forgave him, I soon realized there was another massively important person I needed to forgive, and that person was *me*. This felt so much more difficult than releasing him, but I knew I needed to do it.

I couldn't move on and heal my own internal world unless I used the same compassion towards *myself* that I had in forgiving him. I took the time to continually remind myself that I was also doing the best I knew how during that time. Reminding myself that as I knew better, I would do better. But how could I *know* without the experiences life had offered up to me? It was *through* experiencing these situations that life gave me the clarity to define what I wanted and showed me who I wanted to be. It's this process that has allowed me to be gentle and loving towards myself.

I didn't just apply this tool of forgiveness to myself in dealing with and healing my emotions from this one breakup, but it's a tool I use *all the time* for both big and seemingly small and insignificant situations.

Just the other morning I was at the gym working out. I was setting up at a specific piece of equipment, placing my water bottle and towel on the ground beside the machine when I looked up to see that a lady had squeezed in to use the very machine I was preparing to use. I was instantly annoyed, giving her a less than pleasant look and just stood there. She clearly felt my presence, looked over, and said, "*Oh, were you using this?*"

Snarky, I replied that I *was* using it. She looked uncomfortable and glanced over at her trainer for a cue. The trainer made eye contact with me, said they were almost done and just had one more set. I didn't reply and just rolled my eyes.

I don't know why this irritated me so much, but in that moment it did. What I didn't realize was that they were actually using the piece of equipment and had just momentarily stepped away when I swooped in. We had both thought the other weaseled their way in!

They finished their set and I took over.

About twenty minutes later once I had moved onto a different exercise machine the woman's trainer approached me. I pulled out my headphones to listen to what she had to say. She apologized and then thanked me for letting them finish their last set.

Instantly, I felt both compassion towards her and bad about my reaction at the same time. I had been so quick to get annoyed and to snap at them when here she was being so kind towards me. It had been a simple misunderstanding, and I felt disappointed in myself for failing to see it as such in that moment.

I could've stuck with that emotion and let it take over my day, but instead I chose to practice forgiveness towards myself. I instantly felt forgiveness towards the trainer and her client when she approached me, but I didn't want to internalize my emotion and beat myself up.

As I sat in the coffee shop after my workout, drinking my latte, I closed my eyes, took three deep breaths, and said in my mind, *I forgive you, Katherine.*

Forgiving ourselves is just as important as forgiving others. It doesn't mean you're wrong, it just means you learned. Send yourself love and compassion for the choices you've made that didn't best serve you and for the words you may have spoken that didn't reflect who you feel like on the inside. Send yourself love and compassion, knowing that you did the best you could do *in that particular moment* and if it feels appropriate, suck up your pride and ego and apologize to whomever you need to apologize to.

And then let that shit GO!

Forgiving life situations and circumstances

Even after forgiving myself, as well as those whom I felt had wronged me, I still held a grudge, but this time it was towards my life. This particular grudge was all encompassing. It was directed towards my family, the life I had been born into, and all the circumstances I found myself in that were beyond my conscious control. I had a hard time accepting that which I didn't choose. It's easy to forgive when you're able to move forward to make new empowered choices, but what about the things that are seemingly beyond our control?

Growing up, I was embarrassed and ashamed of my upbringing. I felt like a dandelion in a field of roses. For the most part, my mom raised my brother and me by herself. She was a vegetarian, single mother of two who related to the world with a beyond-her-time hippie sort of mentality. For the first few years, she alternated our education between home-schooling and the Waldorf-schooling system rather than the public school system.

When I did finally go to public school, I remember hiding my lunch from my peers, hoping they wouldn't notice or verbalize the obvious difference between theirs and mine. They had white bread, ham, and cheese sandwiches and packs of sugar loaded Dunkaroos. I had vegetarian tofu chili or a smelly egg salad sandwich served on a slab of bread that resembled a block of birdseed.

I wanted more than anything to fit in with the masses, and not stand out from the crowd. My family made this goal impossible, and I resented them deeply. I wanted to hide them from the world along with my insecure self.

This feeling only worsened as I got older, and the more noticeable the differences between my peers and me became. I was convinced they all knew something

I didn't, and they had been endowed with some gift of which I had been deprived. I was completely convinced they had been set up for success while I'd have to work endlessly into exhaustion to even come close to the same level of accomplishment or acceptance.

I envied the kids who lived in their picture perfect houses surrounded by white picket fences where mom and dad loved each other and would hug regularly, and where sitting down at the dinner table to eat as a complete family was the norm. I also envied the families where the children didn't need to know or understand the concept of money, its deprivation, and the constant struggle to put food on the table and make ends meet. Ultimately, I envied that their lives seemed to manifest with ease, whereas I felt like I struggled to have anything I wanted or that I had to prove myself worthy to be given anything.

I hated those kids! I hated them because I wanted to *be* them. I wanted their lives and would hide the reality of my own in their presence, always trying to fib, hoping they would believe I was actually *like* them. My differences, however, blatantly stood out.

Those feelings of being different progressively got worse during my elementary school days, especially after moving to the small town of Westlock after my one-year stay in Japan. The town was a small, farming community in the country where most people and their families had lived for generations. Many of

Westlock's residents had never traveled far from home—if at all. My brother and I were considered to be freakishly different, having just moved from a country the locals couldn't fathom beyond their school textbooks. Instead of being proud of having my mind opened by experiencing other cultures at such a young age, I wanted to sink into the ground and remain unnoticed.

I soon began to wish I had grown up in Westlock from birth just like everyone else. In addition, I began believing my life would've been better if I'd grown up differently than I had. I honestly believed that my life would be perfect if only... [FILL IN THE BLANK]. If only my parents were still married. If only my mom had more money. If only we didn't move around so much growing up. If only I was skinnier, if only I looked different, if only I had more money to buy fancy brand name clothes, if only I dated the popular guy. *Then* my life would be better and I could be happy. *Then* I could fit in without my alien antennas poking through my skull.

My longing to fit in and my confusion about who I was, who I wanted to be, and who the world expected me to be manifested into me partying, drinking, smoking weed, and having promiscuous sex, starting at the age of thirteen. After moving to the big city after grade ten, these behaviors became even more exaggerated with more frequent drinking and heavier drug use. There were many days I could barely get out of bed to get to school because I'd crashed only a couple of hours before—blackout drunk. My refusal to fail was the only thing that kept my grades high, so I continued to coast academically. I was determined to be the best at everything.

What I've now come to understand and believe is that we're born to this Earth to learn and for our soul to evolve. We don't come here to live a picture-perfect life designed by someone else. As imperfect as it feels when we're here, every circumstance, challenge, defeat and success is an opportunity for us to learn what we were born into these bodies to learn. It's not about creating the perfect vision then aiming and striving for it, and, in turn, creating it in perfect order. It's about having the vision and the desire, and then living through everything that comes up on the unexpected journey *towards* that vision. It's the stuff that happens between where you are and your desired outcome that *is* exactly what you need in order to *get* to the desire at all! That's what life is. That's what the living of it is. Sometimes the best shit happens in between the planned out version of what you decided your life *should* look like or maybe even what other people might have influenced you into believing your life should look like.

It's in extreme **contrast** that you're able to decipher what it is you actually want out of life. The unwanted experiences aren't here to get in the way or screw up the path you lined out for yourself. Rather, they're here to force you to get super fucking clear on what you want and where you want to be. They *are* your path.

A person can peddle along in mediocre health and be completely content even though they might not be living to their highest and fullest potential. It might only be the onset of a serious disease when they suddenly gain a strong desire to be extremely healthy, fit, and active. The desire for good health can't be recognized while moseying along through life from this default position. The biggest obstacle though is that most of us get stuck in this phase of the disease or discomfort and accept it as our reality. We hate on it. We reject it. We reject ourselves. We see it as permanent when it doesn't have to be.

When we come to understand this new perspective of forgiving our life circumstances, we can see how these circumstances are actually playing a beneficial role in our lives. The situations that seem so horrible can be reframed as powerful catalysts to push us forward into that which we actually truly want. These seemingly negative situations and circumstances aren't here to punish and torture us. In reality, they're here to move us further than we've ever gone before. They're here to create forward momentum.

It's nearly impossible to view the shit storms of your life in this way if you're still grudgingly angry with them. Like me in the past, your anger could be directed at the life you were born into, your family, your country, your body and its observed "ailments", and more. Is there a way beyond that anger? Yes. Forgiveness is the key. Forgiveness will set you free from the shackles and chains these situations have placed you in. Forgiveness is the missing element that probably no one told you is a total game changer!

Every so-called "flaw" in your life and your body are learning opportunities you carry with you into this world.

Here's an example from my life.

When I was two years old, the bottoms of my feet broke out in a rash-like skin condition that has never been named let alone cured by doctors, dermatologists, or natural healers. Both my father and his father have this same condition, and both of them have never been able to heal it. My entire life I've grown up rejecting my feet, hating them, cursing them, and hiding them.

I've rationalized this condition as a reason I've not been able to maintain a romantic relationship in my life. I've used it as a reason to hide and play small, as well as a reason not to get involved in things that light up my heart like dance and yoga. I've also used it as a reason to keep intimacy at bay within my romantic relationships, and I've used it as a reason why men haven't accepted or loved me. If only I could "fix" this one thing that's wrong with me physically, *then* I'll be loved. Then I can open up and *really* let someone *in*.

The day of a cure has never come, but I've made a different decision... *that* much *is* in my control.

After researching and undertaking every healing modality I could come by with no results, I decided to forgive my skin, my feet, and my father. My dad was absent for a large portion of my life growing up and because this condition came from him, it only gave me another reason to resent him.

After barely speaking to my dad for ten years, between the ages of fourteen and twenty-four, he contacted me in the spring of 2013 from his home in Colorado to tell me he was coming to visit Edmonton and wanted to see me.

He called my cell phone. My brother, who spoke to him regularly, gave him my number. A long distance number popped up on my call display and before stopping to think about who was calling and where from, I answered.

Upon hearing his voice, my throat constricted and stomach flipped in somersaults, threatening to expel the contents of my lunch. All the bitter pent up thoughts and feelings I had suppressed for years came spilling to the edge of my tongue. I fought to hold them back.

My dad and I had almost completely stopped communicating with each other when I turned thirteen at which time I seriously started bumping heads with his wife, Lisa. The last time I had flown to Colorado to visit him had been a breaking point in our relationship. The day before the journey, my face broke out in pimples and blemishes. In humiliation and panic, I made my mom drive me to the store on the morning of the flight to pick up some face wash that would hopefully clear up the puss filled red bumps.

During the week at my dad's place, I diligently washed my skin, morning and night. Lisa began aiming harsh remarks towards me about my washing regime.

"Oh, Katherine," she would say, "You'd better go put your face on before you join us for breakfast."

My dad would then join in with her chuckling.

The words she spat at me, as well as my father's ridicule and betrayal when he joined in, hurt me profoundly.

On another occasion during the same visit, my dad planned a trip into town for the day to run some errands. The four of us, my dad, Lisa, Joe and myself, would then go out for dinner together. I was excited about this mini adventure, as well as to get out of the house and the same day-to-day routine. I showered and dressed myself in the best outfit I had—a pair of flowery board shorts and a red cotton V-neck t-shirt with the word "Princess" handwritten across the front in a felt-like material. I loved that t-shirt! I can still picture it perfectly today over fifteen years later. I walked out of the bathroom after changing and spotted my stepmother. She inspected me from head to toe and then told me I looked like a slut.

A slut!

A thirty-something year old woman calling a thirteen-year-old child a slut!

Until those words tumbled out of her mouth I felt pretty. I felt beautiful. I felt feminine. Once she let the "slut" word roll off her tongue, whatever ounce of confidence I had inside of me went crashing to the floor. I actually felt it leave my body.

When I returned home I told my mom I was never going back and never did. When my dad would call to catch up and see how I was doing, I refused to talk to him. Eventually he stopped asking. In my stubbornness, I pushed him away, but on a deeper level I wanted him to come running after me. I wanted him to come back and be a part of my life. I wanted him to *want* me to be a part of his life. By refusing to talk to him, I was really begging him to come after me with more determination. And as I grew older, that became the pattern with every romantic partner of mine.

So here I was, almost a decade later, with my estranged father on the line telling me that he and his wife were flying into Calgary and would be driving a few hours north to Edmonton the following day. He asked if I would have dinner with them and my brother. I agreed that I would only on the condition that it would be just him and me. I had no interest in reconnecting with his wife.

We met the following evening at my brother's house where he was staying. I picked him up and we drove to a restaurant. I was shaking the entire way. We sat down and I spilled it out. All of it. How abandoned and rejected I had felt over the last ten years! How hurt and devastated I had felt! I wanted and needed to know how he had allowed Lisa to say such awful things to me. I wanted to know why he stopped wanting me to be a part of his life. Why he hadn't come after me when I was angry with him.

My verbal vomit spewed out across the table between us.

He answered that he was only doing the best he knew how at the time, and that he hadn't known how to handle a stubborn teenage girl up close, let alone long distance. He also told me he didn't know how to deal with a wife and daughter that hated each other when he loved them both.

After hours of hashing it out with both of us crying and raising our voices, I told him I forgave him. It was the three most difficult words for my mouth to formulate, but I did it and I meant it. And I still do.

I decided that evening I didn't want to spend the rest of my life hating and resenting him or the family I had grown up in. I couldn't change the choices we had both made up until this point in our relationship and nor could he. But I knew I had a choice in that moment to keep my wall up and push him away once more, hurting only himself and me *more*, or I could decide that the past was just that... the past. I didn't want to die or have my father die with me being left full of hatred and resentment towards him. This wasn't how my life was going to play out and this wasn't where I wanted to focus my energy.

I also chose to forgive the world for the parents I had been born to. I knew on some level that before my soul entered my body, it had chosen to learn the exact lessons I needed to learn. It wasn't anyone's fault.

I've watched my mother and her two sisters do the same with their father—my grandpa. They spent an entire lifetime hating their father, blaming him for the way their lives turned out. I don't deny they attained wounds and scars from their childhood, but they made a choice in their adult lives and beyond to hold this against him and to condemn him for the choices he had made. I didn't want to live with these feelings of resentment.

When I was a young teenager he got sick with lung cancer. One of his daughters refused to see him, and then after his death, refused to go to the funeral. She was so full of bitterness and hatred for the things he'd done that even on his deathbed she refused to heal her wounds. It's been over ten years since his death, and even now she resents him. She still hates him and feels unmitigated anger towards him. Yet, he's dead. He's gone—away from this physical planet. He was her parent in this lifetime. No other. It could be no other way. And yet she still holds onto her rage towards life.

Seeing this helped me decide that I wanted to forgive my father and forgive the circumstances I felt powerless to control, and that I wanted to break the generational patterning that was forming in our family.

And with that I did forgive, not just my dad, but also the skin on my feet, as well as every circumstance in my life that was beyond my control. I chose to forgive my feet by reframing them as the deepest truth of who I am and that if a man, or any person for that matter, sees them they are seeing this deepest truth. They accept me or they don't and it acts as a filter for those that don't. In this way, I've forgiven my skin condition.

Choosing to forgive someone *does not* mean you condone their behavior and choices. It doesn't mean you agree with the choices they made or that you're saying they're "right" in having made those decisions. But what it's doing is breaking the chains that hold you hostage to your own anger and hurt. It's saying that you won't use the life you were born into as an excuse to avoid living into the happiest version of yourself. It's saying that you'll use your life as a platform to propel yourself into fulfillment, happiness and your deepest desires. It's making a decision that your past doesn't need to equal your future and that through the act of forgiving those people who have hurt you, yourself, and your circumstances then you release the grip and set yourself free.

Forgiveness isn't a onetime shot where pent up feelings miraculously and permanently disappear. Rather, think of forgiveness as something beneficial when adopted as a *lifestyle*. Think of forgiveness as a way of living as opposed to something you do a couple times and move on because, on occasion, certain relationships require *constant* forgiveness over a long period of time, depending on the depth of the pain you experienced.

I practice forgiveness also in the seemingly small and insignificant situations in life. It's like a muscle that grows bigger and stronger the more you use it. Often, it's easier to forgive the less emotionally charged situations than the ones from childhood that caused deep-rooted pain and hurt. When someone cuts you off in traffic or a restaurant employee messes up your order when you're in a hurry just close your eyes and silently forgive that person. Build that muscle! Build it strong!

Looking Your Fear in the Eye

It's almost always the people who have hurt and "wronged" us the deepest that are the most vital for us to forgive. It's through this process that we can find healing and set *ourselves* free.

Probably the most difficult step in the forgiveness process is confronting the pain that we might have previously buried. We have to not only acknowledge the situation, but also *feel* the emotion that has us trapped. We simply cannot be freed of what we stuff and bury deep inside us because it's too scary to feel. What we ignore, deny, and shove away only festers and grows inside of us.

Running away from these painful feelings, doesn't make them go away. They usually return tenfold down the road.

This is how I learned this particular lesson.

When I chose to avoid looking for a new place to live until my lease was up, thereby keeping me next door to Keeth after the breakup, I had no choice than to confront the feelings I had driven underground. I had previously always run away from pain and hurt by turning my back on those involved. But this time I couldn't. Physically I couldn't because of where I lived. There was *nowhere* to run and hide.

At first I tried to run by numbing my emotions with drugs and alcohol, but this strategy became unavailable when I made the decision to get sober.

I spent the first few months hating both him and myself for being in the situation. It would have been *so* much easier in the short term to run away by moving elsewhere. This would have allowed me to stew and continue to despise him in the belief that he had fucked things up.

Instead I stayed while he slept a stone's throw away. I began facing all the emotions of not only *this* failed relationship, but *every* failed relationship of mine. The pain bubbled up from deep within, rising to the surface. It was a conglomeration of the pain of being rejected by all the different men I had been in a relationship with.

I was forced to face the reality of my worst nightmare and fear. It stared me in the face every time I saw a girl park her car outside of his house, screaming to me that he had chosen her over me. Screaming that I wasn't good enough... again.

Okay Rejection... I was listening.

I was finally listening.

I didn't run. I showed up. I gave up on the cat and mouse game I'd been playing with Rejection my entire life.

What do you want, Rejection? What do you want from me? What is it you want to say that's so important you've been chasing me my entire life?

Rejection spoke, "I can only visit you when you abandon yourself."

"What...?" I stammered.

"You heard me. No one can reject you unless you've already rejected and abandoned yourself first."

Okay. *Okay.* I saw it and I heard it. I *felt* it. Finally, face to face. No more hiding behind corners, threatening to jump out and attack me. There I was. And there was Rejection. Looking right at me—deep into my soul.

I thought I had a handle on rejection until it snuck back up on me. Or rather, I snuck back into abandoning myself when I met a new guy. I believed I had acquired an excellent understanding of what a good girlfriend should be, and I was determined to be it in this relationship.

A short six months after I fell for him, he expressed to me that he felt we were more friends than romantic partners and then broke up with me.

Again, I felt beaten. He hadn't felt *that* connection with me. Failed. Failed again at being a companion. A girlfriend. A sexual partner.

I went through a barrage of emotions again... despair, pain, and hurt. I began blaming him for not being what I wanted him to be, and for not loving me the way I wanted to be loved. Yet again I traveled down the road of hating myself and blaming myself for not being what he wanted me to be and what I *wanted* to be for him and for myself.

I began going through the process of writing, praying, and energetically forgiving him and myself over and over again.

I felt like it was the Universe refining the path I was on. It was not telling me I had failed and hadn't made any progress since my last relationship, but quite the opposite. I was being shown just *how* far I'd come. How much I had healed. This was just another process to refine my healing, and to help me understand the fine detailed workings of my life. The fact that I was only in this relationship for a short six months, rather than a few years, confirmed to me I was learning at an accelerated pace.

I had an opportunity to return home to myself and to gain the understanding that this time I hadn't strayed quite as far as I had on every other occasion. I walked away with a more refined understanding of who I was, who I wanted to be, and the areas of my life that deserved attention and healing.

In my own time and in my own way, I thanked this man for showing me the parts of myself I had abandoned. My sexual self, my feminine self and the goddess within me. This time I embraced those parts through journaling and prayer in my own time and on my own terms.

Again, I forgave myself for abandoning me, and for thinking it was his responsibility to draw out of me the parts I had denied within myself. I forgave myself for being scared to be intimate, and for also thinking I had done something wrong. I forgave myself for thinking I had screwed up.

I began to understand the relationship had served its Divine purpose, and that it had run its course. Even through the hurt and the pain, I was able to move forward and polish the areas within myself that I recognized needed polishing.

I felt the pain. I felt the rejection. I felt the hurt, the fear and the agony. I felt it all.

I felt through it. And even as I experienced it I knew I would be okay and that I *was* okay.

Self Reflection Exercise

Forgiving others

A letter of *truth*:

- Think of the person or people you feel the most negative emotion toward. The person who makes you feel the angriest, the most resentful, sad, pissed off or whatever intense emotion you feel when you think of them. That's the person you want to focus on forgiving

- Write "Dear [FILL IN THEIR NAME]" at the top of a piece of paper

- Write them a letter. In this letter spill out *everything* you want to say to them. Don't worry, you're not going to send them the letter, so say *everything* you stopped yourself from saying to them face-to-face

- Get HONEST. Yell all the words of anger and sadness you've felt towards them, cry and tell them everything they've done that has hurt you. Let it all out!

- It's important to examine these feelings—to allow them to come forward and be felt in a safe environment where they aren't going to hurt you further *or* hurt the other person.

A letter of *forgiveness*:

- When you've finished writing this letter, take a clean, fresh piece of paper and write that same person's name at the top

- Continue to write, "I forgive you for..."

- Write down *all* the things they've done that have hurt you—that you *forgive* them for

- As you write down forgiving them for each of these hurt feelings envision a crusty layer built up around you flaking off and being blown away into the wind where it disintegrates—let these past hurts and emotions be washed away from you.

Forgiving yourself

- Continue the previous steps above for both the letter of truth and the letter of forgiveness but this time towards *yourself.*

Forgiving life situations and circumstances

- Continue the previous steps above for both the letter of truth and the letter of forgiveness but this time towards your *life circumstances.*

When you've finished writing the letters, **burn them** (IN A SAFE PLACE!). This releases the energy and emotion in them.

Chapter 10:

Layer 3 – Follow Your Guidance

Ever since I can remember, I've been observing people and how they move through life. What they say, how they act and what they're interested in. I've watched and I've listened. I've always been particularly fascinated with people who are successful—that is, the people who seem to have their shit together! The ones who seem to be abundant, happy, healthy and confident. Although my definition of success has shifted many times over the course of my life, I've always wanted to be the best at whatever I was doing, including living a full life.

I would look at these people who appeared to be thriving and happy. *What* were they doing that I wasn't? *How* were they happy? *What* were they doing that was making them successful? *How* did they *know* what to do?

I had a difficult time trying to understand why they possessed supposedly intangible qualities or resources that I didn't, and why I couldn't seem to access them. I felt frustrated. It seemed to me they had been born into this world with a life manual of sorts, whereas the cosmos had seemingly forgotten to equip me with it or deemed me unworthy of receiving it on the way into my body. But since I didn't have it and they apparently did, I came to the conclusion I would need to figure things out for myself.

I wanted to get it right. I wanted to understand. I wanted to be good at life and I would do whatever it took.

And so began the chase—the chase for happiness, fulfillment, and ultimately, love.

As I grew into my adult life and having interacted with many different types of people through my work as a hair stylist, I started to see that many of the people I'd been looking to for guidance had absolutely no clue what they were doing either! The more questions I asked, the more I observed that nearly everyone seemed to be just bumping along with no real understanding of what was driving them to make certain decisions. But more importantly, I began to comprehend that people weren't *happy*. The ones I had looked to for guidance and direction in order to fill the void in the center of my being were also painfully battling many parts of their lives.

Maybe they didn't have the life manual I thought they had after all. Maybe they were just as clueless as I was. But why were they settling for this struggle? Waking up every day and disliking the life they were living. Working endless hours into complete and utter exhaustion just to reach that sought after day off. Hating every minute of working just to make enough money to book that beautiful vacation only to return to the struggle a week later.

Was this how it is? Was that really how it would be? I wondered when I would "grow up" and figure out what made a life happy and successful. It worried me that the older I got and the more I observed the people around me, I noticed I wasn't the only one looking for these answers, and age was no factor in answering them.

School was a struggle for me. I thought if I could just make it to the light at the end of the tunnel then I would be free and happy. But once I got there the light moved further out of my reach. Surely I hadn't suffered through all those years of schooling just to reach another level of misery. And the worst part was that other people seemed to accept it. So many people I interacted with appeared to not only hate their lives, but also accepted that this was just the way life was! I was determined not to live like this. No more.

If all these so-called "successful" but miserable people didn't know the way forward then how was I supposed to learn? Where were these answers to the success, happiness, joy, peace, and love I was so deeply desiring and longing for?

Surely *someone* had to have the answers!

The Roadmap of Life

There are no set of rules and guidelines that apply to everyone. There's no guidebook that outlines how to live this life successfully. There's no guaranteed action that prescribes happiness. What there *is* though is a guidance system that we're all born with. Our own individualized map known as the Roadmap of Life. We all have one. But each of ours is different.

It's my hope that if more people comprehend they're equipped with a map, as well as how to read and follow it, the world will become a more peaceful place. People will have more fun, laughing, playing and feeling joyful in their own lives. They'll feel more fulfilled and *purposeful*.

The beautiful thing is that we aren't all born into this world to live out the same destiny. We aren't all *meant* to walk down the same path. What creates success and happiness for one person could be exactly what makes the next person completely miserable. That's why we can't follow some generic fulfillment formula like society might have us believe. There's no one right way. There's only the right way for *you*. Only *you* can know what that is. But I can help you figure it out. I can help you because I had to navigate figuring it out in my own life by living through it, and by making constant detours off my path and then rerouting, so I could get back on track.

No two people on this entire planet are the same. Each and every one of us is meant to leave a different mark on this world. We all have different pathways to walk and different destinies to play out. Even identical twins don't have the same fingerprint! The same is true for the fingerprint *we* are to leave on the world. Since no two of us are the same, it must be true that there's no specific guidebook that can be accurately applied to everyone's life. How can someone else who isn't standing in your shoes, and never will be, tell you what your success formula will be?

Yet this is what society teaches us while growing up. It's taught directly, as well as subtly through subliminal messages from the media and our surroundings. In school, teachers provide us with the success formula... we must go to post-secondary and complete X, Y, and Z to have a "good" life. However, what they don't know is the definition differs from person to person.

I'm here to tell you that most everything told to us was wrong. But you already know this don't you? You already feel the discord within your own life from trying to live it to someone else's standard. Something has always felt "off". Like you weren't *fully* and *truly* being yourself.

It's okay. I've been right where you're standing. There *is* another way.

Our Roadmap of Life has an internal compass, which can be broken down into three different components. They are our:

1. **Passions** and **Is-ness,**

2. **Desires,** and

3. **Intuition**

Internal Compass

Passions and Is–ness

What is "passion?" What does it mean?

Growing up we were taught to "find our passions," as if they are something we intend to seek out and identify. These passions, therefore, translate into an activity that we enjoy doing and which we will eventually master. While this isn't a bad thing *necessarily*, it seems to suggest a small and narrow-minded scope that encompasses all of what a passion is and should be. And where does this leave the children and even adults that feel like they aren't good at anything? That is, the people who have a difficult time mastering any particular sport, art, or academic subject?

Well, I can tell you where it leaves them… It leaves them feeling like a total and utter failure at life as they search around trying to find the "thing" outside of themselves they are good at! It also has them seeking *where* they fit in within a community of like-minded people.

But what if passion was something else entirely? Or rather, what if it was something *more* than the distilled version of the one thing we're good at?

Oxford Dictionary defines passion as a "strong and barely controllable emotion." I would like to draw attention to the "barely controllable" portion of this definition and focus on that.

Barely controllable.

It is what *is*.

It's so engrained within your being that you can't possibly *control* it. It *is* who you are. You can't control who you are. We can have great control over the choices we make and the action we take as we move through life, but we have no control over *who we are* on a core and soul level. This is the blueprint our soul came with into our body when we entered the world. It's unchangeable.

I believe our spirit chose this life before we were born even though the conscious mind may not always think this was a choice. I believe there is our truest self—the self we feel like on the inside that's the person and being who we really are. Our authentic self. I also believe, however, that we can stifle our true nature and shape our life and ourselves around who we think we're meant to be rather than who we really are. This, in turn, creates a deep internal conflict between our true self and who we are showing up as in our lives— how we're presenting ourself to the world.

The true self is an intangible and untouchable force that dwells deep within. It requires no explanation, justification, or defense. It just *is*. This principle can be better understood with a gay or transgender person because the difference can actually be seen between what they appear to be and who they feel they are. For the rest of us though, it can be more difficult to pinpoint because it doesn't necessarily have an outward appearance. We can't recognize what it is because it *is* us.

So we're sent off to scour the crowds for people who are "doing things" that we're "passionate" about, so we can link up with them. But we can't recognize what *is* us by searching *outside* of ourselves for it.

How did this knowledge reveal itself in my life?

Since I was young, I've involved myself in numerous activities, teams, clubs, and organizations in an attempt to find what I loved doing and to discover what my passions are.

In elementary school it was the soccer team. In junior high it was drama class, the performing arts, and dance. In high school it was the sports teams and partying. In my adult life once I quit using drugs and alcohol, it manifested in different forms such as fitness, yoga, nutrition, dancing, and different spiritual groups. I'd move along from one thing to the next, trying to love it and to make it who I was. What was I *passionate* about?

And then I had my "Aha!" moment!

When I quit drinking, smoking and doing drugs in my early twenties I needed somewhere to focus that energy. I needed something to *do* that replaced the activities that had been detrimental to me yet had dominated my life. This realization led me into the world of fitness and training. And when I'm in, I'm *all* in!

I hired one of the best trainers in the city and worked with him to develop a food program for me where I was calculating and tracking the food I ate each day. I also followed a carefully constructed workout plan for each day. Every week I would check in with updates on my weight, measurements, and progress pictures.

It didn't take long before I absolutely hated this life-style, finding every way imaginable to sabotage the strict plan I was following. Every weekend I would go on a food binge and then over-train every day during the work week in an effort to make up for the "mess ups" I'd made the weekend before. It was torture. I hated every minute of it. And I felt lost. I beat myself up when I didn't follow my program one hundred percent accurately, and what had started as something I enjoyed doing and felt *passionate* about, quickly became something I was using destructively against myself.

After much agony, I finally made the decision to drop my trainer and my program, and then dived head first into pole dancing. Dancing was what I was passionate about! It's what I did as a kid growing up. It made me feel free and expressive in my own body. *That* was what I wanted to master. So off to pole dancing classes I went. *Four* per *week*! While I loved pole and enjoyed the female connections surrounding it, I again began feeling like this was not *who* I was. I'd look at the instructors and watch endless YouTube videos of the pros and compare myself to them, thinking, this isn't who I am. After recognizing this pattern, I was able to cut down the number of classes I was taking and to enjoy the experience without making myself feel like I had to master pole dancing to be involved. Eventually, I also started working with a trainer, and integrating a food and exercise program into my life again, but in a much more balanced and sustainable way.

All this left me with some serious questions...

Like... *who the fuck am I*?

If I'm all the *things* I'm so *passionate* about then why do I *still* feel unfulfilled? And if I'm defined by all the things I'm passionate about and these things keep changing, who am I really?

I still didn't feel like these labels fit who I was. I enjoyed doing them. I liked dancing and the challenge it presented me when we were taught a new move in class. I liked working out, pushing my body to be stronger and getting a good sweat on, and I also loved learning about nutrition and experimenting with making healthier versions of delicious recipes I enjoyed. But these things didn't feel like my life's purpose!

All this made me feel like *giving up* trying to figure it all out! I didn't want to label myself as anything other than who I was! So I did. And that giving up was the best thing that ever happened to me.

I stopped forcing myself to work out just to look good, to go to dance classes just to be sexy, and to yoga classes just to be spiritual. I stopped *forcing* myself to become the things I was using to identify with because these *things* weren't who I was. They were just that—things. Activities. Vehicles for keeping my body healthy.

I dropped all the "shoulds" I'd been forcing upon myself.

I surrendered to who I felt like on the *inside* even though I couldn't find the labels to describe who that person was on the *outside*.

Who *was I*?

I gave up trying to be who I thought I *should* be, and what I thought I *should* be passionate about. And I just started being. I started following the impulses that came from within me that were spurred from the silence of shutting off the outside world and listening to my inner world. This was a knowing. A natural act of showing up and being in the world.

I've always come up against problems in my life, as we all do, when relationships fail, after getting fired from a job, when feeling sexually inadequate, when losing friends, when encountering death and betrayal and more. Each time I come up against something like this, I would go searching for answers on how to overcome the situation and the feelings I was experiencing. I wanted to know what aspect of myself had caused the discord and how I could transform and heal that part of myself. I want to become better and understand more about myself all the time. I'm fascinated at how life works, my own behaviors and what causes me to have those behaviors. Are they serving me or aren't they? If they aren't, how can I *transform* them into something that *does*?

I look back at my life and see that *this* is my passion. *This* is who I am. It's unchangeable and completely unconscious. I don't try to be it. I don't go looking outside of myself at other people to try to figure out how to become that. I just live my life being me. The "barely controllable." The **Is-ness**.

Is-ness isn't something you go out to become and to master. It's just who you are. We all have it. We all have Is-ness. We just haven't been taught about it until now. We don't know how to recognize it. Our Is-ness controls everything we do, who we are, and how we show up in the world. And it shows up differently for all of us.

Your Is-ness is what guides you to do whatever it is you do. The problem is we've been so trained by society to create a structured life according to everyone else who came before us and who's around us that we don't even know where our Is-ness can lead us. Most people are so completely cut off from their Is-ness. It's hidden in the shadows, trying to come out and play!

What is your Is-ness? It's okay if you don't know right away or if you can't put words to it and it doesn't fall into a certain activity or "doing" action. You can feel it. And that's what's most important. To feel your Is-ness every morning when you wake up and roll over in bed. Feel it and ask it to guide you throughout your day. Let it take the reins. It'll show up and guide you in a serious and powerful way.

My Is-ness came through to me in the conversations I loved having with my hairdressing clients. Coloring and cutting someone's hair became boring and mundane to me. I thrived on the conversation. I started noticing how much I lit up when people began talking about the intricacies of their lives including all the dark corners and the blissful miracles. However, discussions about everyday stuff did nothing for me. They drained my energy. I wanted to get to the bottom of what was causing people pain and help guide them out of it. I didn't even realize that this was exactly what I had been doing all these years under the guise of a hairstylist.

My Is-ness led me to my current vocation, which really doesn't feel like "work" at all because I spend my time doing what I love and want to do, feeling peaceful and blissful, and in love with my life while helping others transform theirs into something that feels amazing for them too.

This excites me. It lights me up, and it makes me feel whole. It was something I had to find by looking within myself for guidance rather than to the outside world for direction. There were action steps to bring it forward after a life of ignoring it, but we'll get more into that in the next chapter.

Desires

For so long as I was growing up, I saw my desires as things I longed for, but would never have. I thought the fact I desired them and didn't already have them meant I wasn't going to achieve them.

As I lived through my life's experiences, I've learned the exact opposite is actually true!

Our desires are within us because they *want* to be manifested. The very fact that we *have* a desire means that it's able to manifest. Rather than a feeling of, *I want it but don't have it*, a desire is really a signal from your true self, which is saying, *I want it and can achieve it!*

The really cool thing when talking about desires is that not everybody has the same ones. If each and every one of us were to write out the best life we could possibly imagine for ourselves, no two people's descriptions would be exactly the same. This very fact demonstrates to us that desires aren't something that are imposed on us from the outside world, but rather something that is birthed from *within* us.

Our desires are there for us to use as a guide, taking us down the road of our best life and truest self. They are giant crumbs left along the pathway of our life purpose, guiding us step by step towards our most fulfilled life.

For myself, I felt a lot of shame, guilt, and embarrassment about my desires for a long time. I'm not even entirely sure why I felt this way. Maybe because I didn't see or hear anyone else around me expressing the same wishes, and because I looked to the outside world to guide me, I thought these desires weren't viable or that there was even possibly something wrong with me for yearning for them.

Your desires are yours and yours alone whether they're the type of work you want to do, the body you want to achieve, or the type of relationship you want. They're within you so you can move towards them. Otherwise, what would be the point?

I've often experienced difficulty in working for someone else and following a work/time schedule they had dictated. I'm a free spirit and, while I work hard, I've always had a desire to work on my own schedule, taking lots of time for self-care, rest, and rejuvenation. The old me thought this wasn't feasible or that I was even a little selfish or crazy to desire such a thing. As I step more and more into living a career based on my deepest life's purpose, I see where this desire was guiding me all along.

I'm meant to run my own business centered on life coaching, writing, and speaking. This doesn't follow the same schedule every day, which reflects my exact desire. It was implanted within me so I could live out and fulfill my divine life purpose.

I've always had a desire to talk through, as well as share my personal experiences. I was never really sure where this desire came from exactly, but I knew that every time I was processing something big in my life, that I wanted to share it publically through my blog or social media. Despite the fear of stepping out and being "seen," I felt this strong urge from deep within me. Again, this is part of my life's purpose to share my journey and processes of self-analysis to help other people love themselves deeper and craft a life around their true self rather than who they're told to be.

Not everyone has the same wish! Our desires are very deliberately placed inside of ourselves for us alone to follow.

What do you *desire*? Speak it out loud and *own it!* Every desire you have is achievable no matter if you've seen example of it in your outside world or not.

The beautiful thing is that when you really start to own your desires, you'll start to notice evidence in your outside world of how that actual desire can be achieved. When I started desiring to be an author, speaker, and teacher, I started coming across other leaders in this field, be it through social media or in real life, that were *already* living this dream I had. Rather than looking at them and figuring that they could do it, but I couldn't, I saw this as evidence from the Universe that not only were my desires feasible, but that they were already being manifested.

Your desires are gifts from your true self to your physical self, guiding you on what actions to take along the way of crafting your best and most fulfilling life.

Intuition

Intuition is a term that gets thrown around a lot, but do we truly understand it and are we really using it to the best of our ability to benefit our own lives and the wellness of the world?

The most common name or definition for intuition is "gut feeling" among others. It is used to describe an inner intelligence that seems near impossible to define. I call it a number of names from my "intuition," "guidance," "gut feeling," a "nudge," or oftentimes I describe it as a "knowing." Whatever name we use, we're all talking about the same inner intelligence.

This knowing has absolutely no logic or reasoning behind it. It usually makes no sense at all. Not only does it not follow the rules of rational thinking, but also it defies logic. This can make it feel uncomfortable to follow in a world where we're programed to follow certainty—where we want cold, hard, logical facts to determine our actions.

I experience my intuition as a deep pulling or urge from the pit of my stomach. Sometimes it feels like a command from something within me that seems to have a gentle authority. Not a mean or rude command, but a command none-the-less. It comes in the form of a clear statement of direction telling me where to go or what to do. It's stern and clear. The only thing that fogs its message is my own mind wanting to disagree or demanding evidence on why I'm being guided in that particular direction.

Intuition is the language of the heart and soul, which is the exact opposite as the language of our mind and thoughts. The two often find themselves in battle with one another. You receive a nudge from within, telling you to do one thing, while your mind convinces you to do the opposite. The mind wants to approach things with logic and with reason while intuition speaks in a peaceful and calm yet authoritative manner with no reasoning behind its directions.

Because we grow up in a world that leads with the mind in the form of intelligence and thinking, intuition is often disregarded because there's no science in the form of fact or data to back it up. But I assure you it's the most accurate directive of all. It's right one hundred percent of the time. Should you choose to follow its messages, it'll *never* lead you astray. It's an intelligence far beyond the scope of human imagination, connected to the entire Universe—past, present, near and far. It operates from a broader perspective than what we can see from the limited perspective of our bodies and lives on Earth.

Following and listening to your intuition requires *trust* that you are being led in the direction of the best outcome for not only yourself, but for everyone involved. With this trust comes also a faith that only good can manifest and result from following your intuition. And with it comes another kind of trust... a quiet understanding that despite all the reasons why you *shouldn't* follow what you're being guided to do, that by paying attention and tuning in, you'll be shown what to do next. As you walk forward your intuition will reveal the pathway one step at a time.

I've often exhibited the need to feel in control of my life, as I think many of us do. I like to figure things out and to have a plan. I like to see the steps laid out in front of me and check them off one by one as I accomplish them. When I have a plan, I have no difficulty pushing the pedal to the metal and plowing forward. I'm a results driven person and have been known to put in a lot of work to get my desired outcome.

While this quality has served me well in many areas of my life, it has also been my opponent when it comes to my intuition. I tend to make a plan and even when my intuition guides me elsewhere. I've often dismissed it when its guidance doesn't calibrate to my original plan. I get into a mental battle between head and heart, going back and forth about what to do. I've spent a lot of time analyzing and questioning why I get into these internal conflicts, and came to realize I only get stuck when my intuition gives me direction and I don't follow it immediately. When my heart pulls me in one direction, but logic creates internal conflict when it tries to "figure out" the best thing to do.

Intuition isn't something that can be "figured out." Ever. Period.

It's been my experience that intuition speaks to us on all topics from the day-to-day mundane activities to the major life choices that can change the trajectory of our future.

There was an occasion when I lived with my brother and another roommate, and I was washing several loads of laundry in the morning before work. That morning I was getting ready to rush out the door, but figured I had time to throw in one more load of whites. I ran downstairs, but something within me told me not to put in that last load.

That makes no sense, my head piped up, *If you just throw in this last load, then you're done.*

I just wanted to finish it, so I could relax later after a busy day at work. So I threw in the last load.

I came home that night after work, and my room-mate told me he had taken my pillows out of the wash and put them on top of the dryer so he could do some laundry.

Oh shit, I thought, *He hasn't seen the other whites underneath the pillows!*

Then a picture of tie-dyed shirts flashed through my mind. I ran downstairs and sure enough I pulled out his wet dark clothes to find my white shirts on the very bottom of the washer. Miraculously, my white clothes were only mildly stained.

The point is, I had a gut feeling guiding me not to do something and I did it anyway. There was a reason I was being shown not to continue with that last load. This is a great example of how our intuition works to make the simple activities of the day flow with more ease. It's not a life and death scenario, but it could have been more harmonious had I followed my intuition!

A couple weeks after the laundry incident, I was driving to the gym to meet a friend for a workout after work. As I drove down the highway, I felt a nudge to take the next exit even though this wasn't the quick-est route to the gym. Without a moment's thought or hesitation, I took the exit and proceeded on my way. When I got to the gym, I parked, then texted my friend to tell her I'd arrived. She replied, saying she was stuck in serious traffic and wasn't sure when she would make it.

When she finally did arrive, some thirty minutes later, she said she got stuck behind an accident as soon as she exited the highway. It just happened to be the same exit I usually take to get to the gym, but had avoided that day.

Aahhhaah! I silently thanked my intuition. Maybe my intuition was guiding me to the different than usual route to the gym to save me the hassle of a traffic jam, or maybe it was a more serious guidance that was keeping me safe and protected from being the vehicle *in* the accident. Either way, I'm glad I followed my guidance.

It's important to note that when following our intuition, we don't always get to see or understand *why* it guided us in a particular direction. For instance, if I had followed my inclination *not* to put in that final load of whites that morning, I wouldn't have known that my roommate was going to put in a load on top of them.

Similarly, I had a friend describe to me an evening where she was to attend a friend's fortieth birthday party. She was preparing to hit the road for an hour-long drive in a rainstorm when suddenly a tree fell across the driveway, blocking her way out! Then an electronic gate from another exit point on her property malfunctioned. She took this as a sign from the Universe that she was meant to stay home that night. Maybe the Universe was protecting her from a potential car accident? Unfortunately, she'll never actually know for sure.

It's not our job to understand *why* we are guided in a particular direction, but to trust that our inner intelligence and intuition *knows* what's best for us, as well as what will serve our highest good in any particular situation.

Intuition is an amazing tool that when listened to and followed through makes the day run so much easier. It can also create massive transformational changes in our lives. It can lead us to a road of more happiness and fulfillment. It can take us to places we never thought possible in our wildest dreams and can change the trajectory of our lives, pointing us towards amazing things and experiences we might otherwise never have believed possible.

When I'm being guided on the major decisions in life, I literally have chills whereupon goose bumps break out over my entire body. I know that when my body has this reaction I need to pay some serious attention to what I'm being called to do.

About six months after my breakup with Keeth, I kept hearing about Hay House's "I Can Do It" convention that was coming to Vancouver. While I'd heard of this event before in other cities around the world and was familiar with the conference, I'd never been so drawn to it, as I was this time. At least once a day for a few weeks I'd hear something about it or that directly related to it. This was a time when I was less inclined to listen to those inner nudges, so I guess that's why this message was repeated to me *so many* times before I actually paid attention to it.

I finally decided it was too eerie a coincidence that this seminar had been brought to my attention so many times. I could no longer ignore it, and decided to make an effort to look into it. Initially, I wasn't able to get the time off work because one of the other stylists had already asked for leave and usually two of us aren't allowed to be away at the same time. Miraculously, after begging and pleading with my boss, she agreed to let me take the time off after I explained to her how important this was to me.

I started looking into flights to get to Vancouver only to discover the prices were far more than I could afford at the time. I'll never forget calling my mom, needing an ear to hear my disappointment when she almost immediately suggested she check if she had enough Air Miles for a flight to Vancouver. You guessed it… she did!!! And she was more than happy to donate them to me for my trip!

What I didn't realize at the time was how pivotal this experience would be for me. At the seminar, I heard a young man speaking whose work I didn't recognize, but something about him caught my attention. I immediately jotted down his name, looked him up, and started following him on social media.

A few weeks after returning home, I was scrolling through Facebook and came across a post from him, saying he would be hosting his first ever writers' retreat in Bali that coming winter where writers and aspiring authors would complete the first draft of their book or screenplay in just thirty days.

As I read through the website material and watched the video pitch for the retreat, the telltale chills and goose bumps ran their way down my entire body.

I almost immediately applied online, having no idea what I was getting into or the amount of money I was about to invest. After a long application process and a short phone interview, I was told that they would love for me to join the group in Bali! This is where I did, in fact, write and complete the first draft of this book, something I never thought possible, especially in thirty days!

Fast forward to now. Here I am with a published book.

My intuition is what guided me towards that convention in Vancouver. And it wasn't just the convention I was meant to attend. It was a decision that changed the direction of my life. That took me towards living my soul truth, which I was so desperately trying to live yet didn't know how.

My intuition has opened up infinite doors to my happiness and success.

We all have it. Each and every single one of us has an inner voice that has been offering guidance and direction our whole lives. Yet many of us have forgotten what this voice is or only hear it in times of desperation or when there's no time to think against it.

With practice and commitment, this voice can become the primary mechanism through which you make your life decisions. It can be the friend you turn to when you don't know where to go or what to do. It'll never fail or betray you. All you have to do is show up and be willing to not only receive this guidance, but follow through on what you're guided to do. Show up and follow through.

How do you come to understand, know, and trust this voice—this inner knowing? Some people understand it through *hearing* it. Others experience it as something they *see* or *feel*. For myself, I most often experience it through a feeling or hearing.

You develop a deeper knowing and understanding of your intuition by getting quiet. By silencing your mind. By having a willingness to receive its message. It's been waiting for you all along. Waiting for you to show up. Just by having a willingness and commitment to do just that, the voice of your intuition will make itself known to you.

I find the best way to magnify this voice is to practice, practice, practice!!! Ask your intuition questions. It can be simple questions like what direction to take to work or where to find a parking spot at the busy mall. And then simply listen and be *open* for an answer.

I like to ask my intuition "yes" and "no" questions like, "Should I turn down this road?" and I pay attention to the answer by listening with my internal ears and by paying attention to the response from within my belly. Sometimes it's faint with little to no response, which I take to mean it doesn't really matter much either way. But sometimes I get a strong pull one way or another such as a strong urge to turn down one road and not another to find parking. I always listen. Always. The more you ask, the more answers you'll get. I believe that our intuition is always there, directing and guiding us but that most of us have such busy minds and lives that we rarely hear it.

It becomes easier to trust your intuition the more you follow it. That's why using it in situations like finding a parking spot or the perfect dress for a special occasion is a great method to start to develop, stretch, and strengthen your intuition muscle. The more you're able to follow it and see that its guidance benefited you in the smaller, less emotionally charged situations, the easier it'll be to trust your intuition in the bigger decisions of your life.

Another time I use my intuition is when I'm mixing color at the salon for my clients. I almost always use my intuition to help me pick which mix of color will give them what they desire. As a result, I've gained a massive clientele, many who tell me, "You just seem to know exactly what I'm picturing without me being able to find the words to explain it."

Yes. Because I'm tuning into that feeling in my gut that will line up with the best interest of everyone rather than racking my brain trying to dissect every word they're using to describe their perfect hair color.

Throughout your day practice asking your intuition questions. Make it part of your life. It'll soon become second nature. Have a conversation with your intuition! You can do this any time as you move throughout your day's activities. You can have it out loud as a spoken dialogue or within the privacy of your own mind—whatever feels more natural to you!

It's my belief that gut feelings show up strongly and prominently when we're in immediate danger, and where we immediately follow them without time for our minds to argue and rationalize something different. It's also my belief that through practice and development, we can learn to utilize this form of guidance in *all* situations of our life, leading us on a more direct, easy and peaceful route towards our goals and desires.

I have a passion for sharing these tools and information because it's something many of us were never taught growing up. Nobody sat down and explained these systems to us. No one helped us understand that we have these amazing no-fail systems built *into* us... that they're *part* of our very being. Neither were we told that these systems work, whether we're *aware* of them or not, always nudging and guiding us in the direction we were born to go in, helping us out in the minor and major situations throughout the day and the lives we find ourselves occupying.

Where you've felt lost, alone, and directionless you now know you are supported from within. You aren't alone. None of us are. Never forget this. Turn over and over again to your built in guidance systems to show you where to go. It'll never lead you astray. It'll *never* fail you. *Ever.*

However, it's our job to show up and pay attention. To take the time to get quiet, and tune into ourselves and the force working from within. It's a paradigm that will change your life, making it flow with much more ease and grace.

I find the most beneficial way of getting quiet is to spend time alone. It's difficult to hear the intelligence within ourselves if we're constantly bombarded with the external noise around us. It's our job and responsibility to create space within our lives to spend this sacred time to ourselves. You owe it to yourself! And I assure you that you, your family, and others in your life will reap the benefits when you make the commitment to spend time each day alone, reconnecting to yourself and your intuition within.

Self Reflection Exercises

Passions and Is-ness and Desires Exercises

How do you figure out your Is-ness?

This is one of the few times I'm going to suggest going outside of yourself for guidance, but in this scenario it can be extremely helpful! Because our Is-ness is so deeply engrained within us, it can be difficult for us to detect on our own. We can't always recognize *what* we are because we *are* it.

Ask all different people from different arenas of your life from family to co-workers to friends to clients. Any type of person you can think of. Ask them:

- What are your unique qualities and gifts?

- What do they see in you that makes you, *you?*

- Write down the words they use to describe you. Make a list.

I can almost guarantee that amongst these different people, many of the same unique qualities and gifts will show up as their answers, despite many of them not knowing each other.

- Read over your list, taking special note of the qualities that appear multiple times

- Which descriptions resonate with you the deepest?

These are your Is-ness qualities!

Then, think of yourself first thing in the morning. Right when you wake up. The second your eyes open ask yourself...

- What's your first *urge*?

- What do you *feel* like doing?

We're more in tune with ourselves first thing in the morning when our conscious mind hasn't fully taken over, so this is a great time to check in with yourself and really observe what's going on.

- What are your natural impulses at this time of day?

- What makes time seem like it stops for you?

If you didn't have a job or family obligations that felt set in stone each day then:

- How would you spend your day?

Picture it. Waking up with absolutely *nothing* on your agenda for that day. No responsibilities. No bills to pay or money to make. No family to rely on you. No class you have to be at or assignment you have to complete by a certain deadline. No flight you have to catch.

- What would you *do*?

- How would your day *look* and *feel*?

Your natural impulses are the key to your Is-ness.

- What topics of conversations do you most often find yourself in?

- What makes your ears perk up when overhearing another's conversation?

The conversations where you feel yourself totally lit up and engaged! Where even if you were previously tired, suddenly you're invigorated. Where the words seems to just flow from your mouth with effortless ease.

- What's being talked about in these conversations?

This is another massive key to your Is-ness!

- What are your innermost desires?

- The wants that burn deep within your center?

- The things you don't speak because you think they would be too ludicrous for anyone else to hear?

- The things you think outloud that others would categorize as crazy? What are they?

The answers to all these questions whether *spoken out loud*, *written down*, or simply *contemplated*, encompass your Is-ness, passions, and desires.

Intuition Exercises

The most effective way to connect with your intuition is through getting quiet in both your external *and* internal worlds. This requires setting aside the time to spend by yourself away from family, friends, and technology. It also requires an effort to create stillness and peace within your mind. Our minds can seem to have a dialogue all of their own and because of this it'll benefit you to calm this inner conversation and get in touch with what's beneath it.

This can be done through meditation.

- Sit comfortably with either your legs crossed or your feet flat on the floor, keeping your spine straight

- Take a *full* breath, pulling the oxygen *deep* into your belly

- When you can't take in any more air, hold your breath at the top for a couple of seconds and then *release*. Let it go. The breath, your tension, *all* of it!

- Repeat this 3-10 times.

Focusing on your breath keeps your awareness within yourself. It distracts from the commotion of the outside world as well as the commotion within your own mind.

Spend time in nature! Being in the natural environment, connects many people back to themselves. Our minds can often become clouded in the busyness of everyday life, as well as indoor environments with artificial lighting. Reconnecting with nature can be a powerful way to know your intuition deeper. You can do this in a few different ways:

- Go for a walk

- Play with a pet

- If you don't have access to green space outside, bring a plant into your home

- Take your socks off and walk in your bare feet through the grass, sand, or mud.

Practice asking your intuition questions! Having an open dialogue with your intuition can help you to understand this intelligence on a deeper level and make it easier for you to be in touch with the guidance offered up from deep within on a regular basis.

Here are some questions you can ask your intuition:

- Where can I find a convenient parking spot?

- What route will most effectively get me to my destination?

- Should I go on a date with this person?

- What form of exercise will most benefit my body at this time?

- Which restaurant should I eat at tonight?

These are more simple questions where you probably have less emotional attachment to the answers, which is a really great place to start practicing tuning into your intuition. This will help build your trust and confidence in using your intuition for the bigger and more life altering decisions where your intuition is offering you guidance.

Chapter 11:

Layer 4 – Take Inspired Action

Our lives won't move forward unless we do. We must align with what our guidance is telling us. We can be steered over and over again. We can meditate and chant for hours. We can pray for all the help, support, and direction in the world. But... if we don't take *action*, nothing changes and we continue to feel stuck with our wheels spinning in the mud.

There's a reason the action step comes after explaining the guidance system you're equipped with and that's because, in western culture we tend to live in a predominately action-based world. Everything is about pushing forward, driving with force, struggling with blood, sweat, and tears to produce an outcome. It's about sacrifice and hard work. Putting yourself through torture to eventually make it to this elusive destiny you long for.

Well, after having lived my entire life this way and getting quite good at it, I finally had enough of the bullshit cycle of pushing, pushing, *pushing* until the point of burnout and exhaustion. Pushing through the pain.

This isn't how I wanted to live despite the fact it's the only way I knew *how* to live. I hated it.

As mentioned previously, for the majority of my life I grew up with a single mother who struggled, working two to three jobs through my childhood and teenage years to make ends meet and to provide the life she wanted for my brother and me. She did this from the purest intention and a place of great love. She thought she was doing something awesome for us.

Yet, a part of me strongly disagrees.

I modeled this behavior, as it had been modeled by my mother, as well as by *many* other people of influence—I believed I needed to live a life of sacrifice. That I couldn't have my cake and eat it too. That I wasn't meant to live joyously and pleasurably. That I must *earn* the right to feel good and experience freedom. That these blissful feelings only come after working endless hours *for* them. That they only come in *response* to the hard work.

The reality, however, is that feeling peaceful and happy is actually our birthright. *Yes*, that's right. Our birthright. Every one of us not only deserves joy, pleasure, freedom, abundance, bliss, happiness, intimacy, connection, and love, but is also *entitled* to them. They're not our rewards at the end of a miserable workday we fucking hate! Yet, this is the way many people's current existence plays out.

Misery in exchange for abundance. Stress in exchange for the sweet release that comes at the end of the day when you crash on the couch after a day of exhausting work. Overtime worked week in and week out for those seven days of "vacation" where you get to live the life you *actually* desire.

Something always felt off about this to me while growing up. Even when I was caught in the trap of possessing an excellent work ethic, something within me felt wrong. Something felt deceptive—like I was abandoning a *huge* part of myself.

I thought I would earn my freedom after twelve years of torture at school. But as school came to an end and I made my way into the full time work force, I soon felt the torment persisting there too. This came in the form of being on someone else's schedule. It was my boss who decided what time I needed to wake up in the morning, how much money I would make, and when I had put in enough hours that they felt I was deserving of some time off. And the internal agony continued for me.

Don't get me wrong, while I didn't like working for someone else all those years, I was good at doing it. I worked my *ass* off, always wanting to prove to my employers that I was a "good person," as well as a "good employee." What I didn't realize was that I was trying to prove I was worthy. Of *what*, I don't exactly know... maybe to be liked, to be paid, to have time off. Whatever it was, I was trying to prove it.

All the while that I thought I was getting ahead, I found myself feeling worse and worse about myself and continually more exhausted. ALL. THE. TIME.

I was taking action with none of the inspiration. I wasn't following my inner guidance and, therefore, was making no progress towards my ultimate goal of being happy and feeling peaceful.

Something had to change.

I wanted something different than what I was living, but I didn't know where to turn. I didn't know what steps to take to get out of this rat race I called life. And so, I continued for years, not really making any actionable changes, but wishing for something to change. Wishing for a miracle to come and save me from this world I hated being a part of.

The missing component was tuning into my inner guidance and then taking action from the communication that was given to me. You see, just by asking for the help, I opened up my guidance system to come in. However, by not following through with Inspired Action, things stayed the same.

The pivotal moment came when I paid attention to all the signs that showed up and then flew to Vancouver for the "I Can Do It" convention. I had prayed for a shift. The Universe provided an answer, I heard it, and I followed through with *Inspired Action* by booking my ticket and flying to the event.

It was scary for me at the time. I was out of my comfort zone, especially doing it by myself, but I knew I had to go. It was that *knowing* I talked with you about in the previous chapter.

If only it just took that *one* leap of faith into the unknown for everything to miraculously fall into place... No, that's not how it works. Not. At. All.

You must take action *continuously*. It involves getting quiet enough to hear what you need to do and then actually *doing it*. Over and over again... tuning in and following. It's a system to make an implemented part of your entire life. This is a life-long path that over time becomes more and more natural to follow.

Under Action

Under action, simply put, is the passive act of sitting around waiting and wishing for your dreams to manifest. It's doing all the visualization work, but doing nothing when the cues show up for you to get your butt in gear!

I feel this is the area that attracts too much focus in the spiritual world where attention is directed at the energies—what some people see as "woo-woo." Many of these practitioners and teachers tend to ignore the importance of our physical bodies and the physical actions we take have in the equation.

I've been there and I get it. This world is harsh, full of extreme energies and vibrations, and floating out of my body and going to a happier place seems like a good solution to having to deal with Earth at times. While this *is* an amazing tool during meditation and other spiritual practices to bring your Higher Power and Higher Self into full alignment, it doesn't provide a practical way of living full time in our bodies. Wishing, imagining, and visualizing are the first steps to creating the life we want and to becoming self-approved, but it doesn't stop there.

In Under Action, we get constant prompts from our inner guidance system, but more often than not we don't recognize them for what they are, let alone take action. As a result, we start to feel *stuck*, frustrated, and our lives come to a standstill. It can feel like nothing is working in our favor.

The Secret used to be one of my favorite films in my early adult years. It changed my life. It opened me up to the realm of possibilities that I previously didn't think were feasible, introducing tools for introspection I hadn't even known *existed*. Each time I watch it I still feel inspiration pumping through every cell of me.

I spent hours with my eyes closed, *feeling* the way I wanted to feel, visualizing the man of my dreams, even imagining his hands running intimately across my skin, his breath in my ear, his lips against mine. It was after watching the film that I went out and bought a poster board, stacks of magazines, colored markers and got to work building my first vision board. Creating a *visual* of all the things I wanted to manifest. I envied the fitness models with their flat stomachs, toned arms, and muscular butts. Their images plastered my bedroom. I'd stare at them, close my eyes, and imagine myself looking like them and feeling vibrant and healthy. Even though I might not have been able to articulate it at the time, I didn't *just* want a body like these women. Instead, I wanted to *feel* vibrant, healthy, and full of life while *also* loving the way my body looked aesthetically. I wanted to *feel* comfortable and at home in my own body. I didn't want to fuel myself on junk, which just clogged the engine of my flesh vehicle on Earth. I wanted food and nourishment that made me feel ALIVE!

Years passed and nothing really changed with my body. I would lose and gain the same ten pounds over and over again, depending on what I was using at the time to suppress my emotions and deal with life—drugs and alcohol or food. Sometimes it was both. Sometimes it was one or the other. During my hardcore party phases, I was drinking and snorting so much I didn't really care or think about food. Getting high and noticed became my addiction. Then during the times when I was in a relationship and not going out and partying as much, food became my drug of choice and I would pack on extra weight, getting all my pleasure from devouring delicious meals as a way of avoiding really opening up and experiencing plea-sure with my partner.

The point is that even when I was my slimmest self, I didn't *feel* the way I wanted to feel, and my life still wasn't reflective of what I had envisioned it to be or what I'd created on my vision board.

I WASN'T TAKING ACTION!

How was I going to have the body of my dreams if I kept eating deep fried fast food every couple of days while getting little to NO exercise and barely any sleep? I would then look at my body and be frustrated that my life wasn't the way I wanted it to be, as if some higher force outside of myself was supposed to make me do the things required in order for me to be where I wanted to be! I was missing the connection between how I envisioned my life and what I was actually doing day-to-day—this is also why the mindfulness we talked about earlier is so important.

The Universe was, in fact, showing up through the internal nudges I was receiving to get my body *moving!* To get my butt to the gym or yoga class. It was directing me to go outside and walk through nature, to pick up a green juice instead of a diet pop, a carrot instead of French fries. Yet, I was continuing the same behavior that had given me those same results, which were results I had decided I no longer wanted to shape and define my life.

Your dreams can't show up for you unless *YOU show up for YOU*.

The Importance of Faith

It's crucial we learn to trust life. To trust the Universe, God, Creator, or whatever name resonates with you and to trust *yourself*. Life can be scary if we don't feel supported and taken care of. We can often experience a constant state of anxiety and sometimes even terror.

But... and this is a huge *but*... relying on the Universe to have your back is only half of the equation. Well, okay, maybe it's more than half, but it's not the *full* equation. There's a missing piece.

And that missing piece is you. You, right as you are in your physical body, have to line up and fill the missing piece of the equation.

Free will.

No matter what we think our destiny is, our foreseen path, what we're "meant" to become, none of it matters without the free will to show up and take action.

Baby steps. Every single day. Always moving forward and progressing.

Over Action

Over Action is the exact opposite of Under Action.

It's the running, running, running. The scrambling. The feeling of needing to continuously be doing something all the time. It translates into a sense that unless you're *doing* or accomplishing something, you're unworthy, and you're wasting your time. It's a feeling of having to schedule and fill up every moment of your day with something that feels productive.

Productivity is good, but when it isn't in alignment with your guidance and inspirations, you might as well be running around in circles, dying to catch your breath, yet going nowhere.

I myself have been a classic Over Actioner. Going back, I probably learned this from my mom who was the busiest person I know. My model was that when someone asked you how you're doing, you were doing well in life if the answer was, "Oh, I'm so busy!" as if this validated your existence on the planet! Like you have to be doing something to even be worthy of having a good day! I don't think I'd *ever* heard someone say "I'm feeling really peaceful, connected, and so much in my life is synchronizing with my desires right now. It's *awesome*!" This seemed almost socially unacceptable compared to the first response.

Why is that?

The measure of what you accomplish in a day has no bearing on who you actually are or what you're worth and deserve in life. It's just another form of ego having to prove itself and asking you to prove yourself. At the end of the day it's a bullshit liar. It's the deceptive voice in the back of your head telling you that you'll be able to relax and feel good after you finish your mile long TO DO List that needs checking off first. That nothing will fall into place and nothing good can come in your life unless you're constantly working and struggling.

It's the belief that if I'm not struggling, then something's going wrong! I mustn't be on the path to my dreams unless it comes with pain, sacrifice, and heartache.

What if the path to your dreams actually meant following what feels *good* to you? What feels *effortless* and *natural*? What comes with *ease*? Led by the natural *desires* that yearn from within.

After Keeth and I broke up and I decided I couldn't drink my way out of the way I was feeling, I turned to exercise and fitness as a means of coping. I wanted to spend as little time as possible at home. I wanted to run away from him and away from my life. Since I couldn't logistically do this, I ran away through exercising so I could clear my thoughts and diffuse my emotions.

Sweating my ass of at weekly boot camps became my release. My body started changing along with my mindset. I was starting to love the way I looked and felt. The "problem areas" on my body that I thought were unchangeable and unacceptable started to morph in ways I didn't know possible. I wanted more. More of what, I don't even know, so I pushed harder and harder and *harder*.

My workouts became my priority and every day I'd spend two to three hours in the gym meticulously following my workout plan with almost an entire day each week dedicated to carefully prepping, weighing, and calculating my food.

I found myself in a state of *Over Action*, and a feeling of uselessness came over me the minute I wasn't doing something that seemed productive. I had to be *doing* to *be*. Or at least this is what it felt like. Yet at the same time, I never felt like I was making any real progress, running in circles like a hamster on the wheel to nowhere. Even though I was getting the results I desired, I still wasn't *feeling* satisfied. This is because I still wasn't experiencing the internal feelings and peacefulness I also desired.

A lot of people adopt this same pattern with their work. They believe the philosophy that they have to be super busy and exhausted to be moving in the right direction.

Like so many others, I found myself in the same trap, working what felt like endless hours to try and make it to the next bracket of income, barely crawling out of the doors of work by the time the day ended. Ah, but I had earned the mighty dollar, which had been my intention. But "how" I got it wasn't in alignment with the life I wanted, and I felt like it came at the cost of my soul.

There were slow days at the salon where I would only have a couple clients booked and on occasion none at all. This caused me so much anxiety. The worse case scenario played out in my mind… I wouldn't be able to pay my mortgage that month or I would have to cancel my gym membership and borrow groceries. Going broke felt like death to me, and caused my deep-rooted fear to rise.

Of course, this was never the case and even if it was a slow week, it almost always picked up the following one and I was able to pay my bills every single time and have some leftover money.

I equated the lack of money with a certain death. I didn't know how to not do anything at work or in any area of life. It was as if I wasn't doing *something*, I was dying. This, of course, sounds ridiculous in hindsight, but internally, it's how I felt at the time. It's my hope that through the sharing of my experience with over working and fear will help you to look inward and to your current circumstances to see where similar dynamics might be showing up.

Do you take action before feeling inspired? Are you hustling away at work only to bring home a paycheck that hardly satisfies your deepest soul desires? Do you really believe that this is the way we're meant to live out our lives, especially if we're lucky to survive until retirement only to take a sip of living the life we *actually* want? An entire lifetime of sacrifice for only a fraction of that time spent doing what brings you joy. And what many people discover after retirement is that they feel like they don't know what to do with themselves. They've been so used to being busy and stressed, that they can actually re-create those feelings even though the external things that were causing them are gone.

This sounded like a bullshit way to live out my life and, worse yet, it didn't *feel* right. It felt like complete torture. I literally felt my life force energy being sucked out of my soul every time I'd think about living this model of work and life. I would feel like I was surviving off nothing but fumes when I crashed through the front door of my home every night when I was done plowing through the workday.

Yet, everywhere I looked, this seemed to be the way that others were living. And worse still, they accepted it as normal. Many of those people were ones I looked up to as a child and teenager. At the time I thought that once I reached their level, *then* I would finally have it figured out. When I got there, *then* I could be happy. The problem was that as I began doing what I thought I was "supposed" to do and living the life those adults led me to believe was the successful way to live, and I still *felt* miserable!

What was next then?

Well, clearly I thought I could work my way through it. Push my way through it. And after almost ten years of doing this in my chosen career path as a hairstylist, I felt like I was going to break.

I had to stop pushing so hard at work and at exercise if I wanted to experience the internal feelings I desired of peace and fulfillment.

Initially when I stopped pushing so hard, I perceived myself as being weak for giving up and for being unable to step up to the challenge. I was slipping from perfection. Panic ensued, but not for long.

Not for long...

Then something happened. It wasn't immediate. It trickled into my life as a kind of ease and a deep sense of peace. When I let go of what I thought I was giving up, I ended up landing on a most beautifully soft surface that had been there all along, underneath my self-made struggles. As soon as I stopped clinging to them I was set free.

It was the craziest thing for me to intellectualize because it went against everything everyone around me was living and teaching me. It went against what I grew up thinking was the path to a successful life.

In this process of giving up I found what I was looking for all along—peace. There it was right in front of me and right *inside* of me, waiting patiently for me to slow down enough to feel it. I suddenly comprehended that in all this time my quiet nudging voice had been begging me to look in a different direction—an inward direction. It was guiding me to give up the model of the world I had known and to follow the natural inclinations from inside myself.

In my Over Action, I wasn't getting anywhere, but falling further down the hole of misery. And this was a hole I refused to live in. In making this decision, my life changed. It still changes every day. Now every morning I choose peace over anxiety, as well as the path of least resistance, which invariably leads me towards who I am and away from the illusions outside of myself I believed I had to "become" in order to be successful.

There's nothing you have to *become*. You only need to slow down and listen long enough to feel what you already are. You *already* are it. You ARE. It only seems like a contradiction when your mind tries to understand it, but when you *feel* it with your heart you know it's true. You can sense it with your very being.

Will you allow your heart to take precedence over your chattering mind? Will you turn away from what the world is saying you should be, and instead relax into what you already are, amplifying it for the rest of the world to see? And in doing so, give every single person who makes contact with you, direct or indirect, permission to ease into who *they* are as well?

Or will you keep pushing? Fighting? Struggling against yourself? Against the part of you that is eternal—your Is-ness, where Inspired Action flows?

Inspired Action

Inspired Action is the opposite of Over Action *and* Under Action. It's what follows guidance, and it flows with ease when you allow that guidance in because the steps required for you to reach your desired goal or result naturally unfold in front of you—one step at a time.

Just the other day, I was driving to the gym in the morning for a workout and it was extremely foggy. So much so that I could only see about ten to fifteen feet in front of my car. For a moment, I panicked! How could I get there barely being able to see where I was driving? All of a sudden, a flood of wisdom came rushing into my awareness, as if from a source outside of myself, and I thought... I can see ten feet in front of me and as long as I can *keep* seeing ten feet in front of me, I'll get where I'm going. I don't need to see the entire path, but I do need to trust and keep moving forward.

I suddenly understood this as a metaphor for my life. It's something I remind myself of often when I don't know what's ahead. I make a decision to keep moving forward, keep taking action, and trusting that the next action step will be revealed to me as I go.

You'll know when the action is coming from an inspired place because it feels like you have no other choice but to follow through. It feels like a knowing and a truth that seems to speak from inside of you rather than from the outside world. You can *feel* the internal discord when you ignore this call to action and it nags away at you, begging you to pay attention.

Inspired Action feels urgent. Not in the sense that you have to rush to get it done, but in the sense that you have a *duty* to fulfill and the outcome will be *powerful*. When ignored, it continues to urge you, over and over again, until you hopefully respond.

The fact that this action you're inspired to take comes from a place of peace *doesn't* mean it always feels natural or within your comfort zone. In fact, it often feels like it goes against the life you've previously known. Your ego and your head will try to wrestle this inspiration to the ground in an attempt to convince you that you can't do it or that you might even die in the attempt.

Your ego is lying. Your mind is lying. It's how these parts protect themselves from you living large. And so, they try to keep you small because they're under the false impression that by living small you're living safe. While this might seem true, if you comply with this directive by shrinking away and living small then you submit yourself to a slow painful *inner* death.

The actions you're inspired to take will, more times than not, *scare the shit out of you*. The action you'll be required to take will mean you'll confront your deepest fears directly in the eyes. Your fear will scream and implore you to back down. This is normal. Just acknowledge it and *do it anyway*. Fear of doing something isn't a reason to not do it. Often, it's the things that cause us to grow the most and become the best versions of ourselves that feel the most uncomfortable.

The action you must take will feel scary. It'll feel like a stupendous risk because it lies on the outside of your comfort zone and beyond the habitual patterns you've developed in your life up until now. In fact, on some occasions it might demand you act in complete *opposition* of them.

As I write this, it's been almost two years since I shaved my head. I had hair half way down my back. It was long, luscious, healthy, thick brown hair that cascaded over my shoulders. I got complimented on my hair all the time. It was beautiful hair. I felt beautiful *with* my hair.

I was driving home from work one evening, thinking about and contemplating my life as I usually do, when an idea popped into my head. It was actually more than an idea—it was a cause. Chills ran down my spine as inspiration flowed through me.

The idea was to shave my head. However, it didn't just tell me to rush home and grab the bathroom clippers and get to work. There was a message hidden in the idea, which I needed to deliver and share with the world. This message had been trapped inside of me and I couldn't seem to communicate it with words alone. Rather, it was a message I had to demonstrate and to embody. It was a message I had to show rather than to articulate.

I was tired of living my life based on people's belief that only physical appearance counts as value in the world—that it's the only validation of beauty in a woman. I was sick of having an endless line up of people judge me on nothing more than my body and beauty, including my *own* judgments. I was deeper than that. So many other people are too, and I wanted to get their attention to remind them of that.

I'd lived my entire life up to that point of time, assessing and criticizing the way I looked, the shape and size of my body, and how my beauty measured up to everyone else. I spent 25+ years trying to change my body and make it better, as well as feeling I wasn't good enough to be loved. Loved by another and loved from within.

It seemed like I had to become something I wasn't in order to feel good, and that I had to look a certain way or *be* a certain way. Because I thought this about myself it is, in turn, what the world had reflected back to me.

Why was it that when some people looked at me and told me how beautiful I was I would begin to ridicule myself or deflect the compliment? Never feeling comfortable in my own skin, always feeling like I had to lose weight and tone up or be on the quest for bigger boobs, a smaller waist, tanner skin, and whiter teeth. Why was it when I received a compliment, I'd look down at my body or at my face in the mirror and *feel* the opposite?

I strove to be beautiful, but I never actually felt it. Ironically, I made my financial living, making other people look and feel beautiful from the outside when I colored and styled their hair.

So I set off on my mission to show the world that we *aren't* our looks. No matter who we are, we aren't *just* our bodies. We aren't our hair, skin, or weight. We aren't the clothes we wear or the make-up we plaster on our faces. We're none of that. It's a temporary and ever-changing *part* of ourselves.

Wanting to achieve more than just the shaving of my gorgeous hair to share this message, I found a local organization in my city that runs programs for young girls in junior high. It teaches them about personal empowerment, as well as how to achieve high self-esteem and make peace with their body. It was a program actually putting into practice the inspiration I was experiencing.

I called my campaign "Bald for Beautiful," and I set out raising money for the YWCA's girls' programs that helps them develop these positive aspects of themselves and sets them up to become leaders within their community.

When I first started, I didn't really know what I was doing, but I felt a call to action that was loud, clear and concise. I followed it without hesitation, figuring out each step along the way as I moved forward.

Aside from the money I was raising, I wanted to demonstrate to *all* women that their beauty radiates from within, and that it doesn't matter what size their breasts are, how many wrinkles they have on their face, or what size jeans they wear. I felt this message brewing inside me for years. It didn't convert into something tangible that I actually lived every day until I tuned into my inner guidance and followed through on it—*Inspired Action.*

Scared is an understatement of how I felt when the clippers came towards my head, but it was something I knew I had to do from within my soul. The call came from a deeper place than the superficial hair I was hacking off.

I organized to have the head shave event at the salon where I worked, selling tickets in advance to my family, friends, and clients. More than fifty people showed up that evening to cheer me on, their eagerness fueling me further, even as my nervousness threatened to take over.

The room filled with people, and I got ready to say goodbye to my hair and, with it, my old beliefs I had associated with my physical looks. I was shedding more than the physical weight of my hair, and I could feel that truth in the pit of my belly as my emotions heightened.

My hair was tied into little ponytails all over my head. My mom cut off the first one and the girls I worked with cut the others in succession. As my head began getting lighter, my emotions began getting heavier and heavier.

I felt like crying—not because I was sad to be losing my hair, but because I was so overwhelmed with inspiration. It's like I could feel all the life force of the Universe pumping through each cell of my body in that moment. I felt *on purpose*. A high I never came close to reaching through alcohol or cocaine. It was a high fueled by my mission.

I felt the cold clippers glide across my scalp and watched what little hair remained on my head, fall to the floor around me, lighter and lighter, old parts of me falling to the floor along with my hair strands.

I looked up and into the eyes of all the people watching me. Some were crying, others gasping, and some were whispering, "Oh, she's so brave." I felt elation in my heart, as I *knew* I wasn't just doing this to free myself, but to free every other woman who had ever experienced similar feelings of not being good enough.

As my co-worker finished up shaving, the ladies from the YWCA tallied up all the money that had been raised through ticket sales, silent auction items, and cash donations. When I stood up to see my new reflection in the mirror in front of me, they presented me with a giant check, totaling over eight thousand dollars! I was overcome with inspiration and tears as they told me this was enough money to send nine girls through the program.

Never before that moment had I felt so on purpose.

Under Action, Over Action, and Inspired Action. They all produce some sort of result, but only one will produce a result in total harmony with the life you imagine yourself to be living—the life you deeply *desire* to be living.

Inspired Action won't always make sense. It might actually even defy logic, but that doesn't matter. What matters is that you stop, listen and tune in, then follow through no matter *how* scary it is.

No one can tell you if your inner guidance system is accurate. Only you can know this, and you know it by *feeling* it.

Over Action can most definitely create success, but what's success without fulfillment at the forefront? It's the combination of achieving your individual success goals, as well as feeling out and following through on the action you're inspired to take that truly creates a life of bliss, joy, and peace.

Self Reflection Exercises

Get out there! When we take action and try new things, it shifts the energy in our lives and brings new opportunities towards us—it's important to start *somewhere*.

- Is there something that interests you, but that you've never actually gotten out to try like yoga, dance, painting, or cooking classes? Maybe there's a little boutique store you've always wanted to check out, but never made the time to stop and go in?

- TAKE ACTION – go *do* the thing you've been wanting to do, but haven't committed to in the past.

Create a vision board

You're going to create a vision poster of all these things and feelings you wish to acquire.

Write down everything that you *want* in your life in the following categories (go big!):

- Health

- Relationships

- Career/work

- Finances

- Focus not only on the end result that you want to see in each of these areas, but how it *feels* to be living your desire

- Look through magazines and cut out phrases and pictures that represent what you wrote down. Google image specific pictures that also correlate

- Tape or glue all the different images onto a piece of poster board. You can do this in whatever fashion best suits you—maybe that's collage style or maybe that's having everything neatly in sections for each category. Just do what *feels* best for you

- Hang this poster board somewhere you're going to see it every day—maybe in your bedroom or office.

These are going to be the desires that inspire your action. It's important to pay attention, especially over the coming days and weeks to the thoughts and ideas that seem to randomly pop into your head. This is your inspiration so when you feel called to take action, do it! Even when it feels like out of the ordinary and even if it doesn't seem like it would directly relate to your desired outcome. Often we can't see where our actions are going to lead us so it's important to follow it when the inspiration comes.

Chapter 12:

Layer 5 – Let Go!

There's something incredibly valuable I believe every person would benefit from knowing and understanding. This one thing has absolutely changed my life, causing it to continually move forward with ease and grace. It's the one thing I turn to when I find myself tensing up or feeling stressed with what's going on in my life or how I think other people and even how I'm perceiving what's taking place.

It doesn't require physical exertion. It doesn't require going out and acquiring some sort of schooling or degree. You can do it from wherever you are—no matter where that is. It's available to you in any and every moment.

This one thing is *letting go.*

Growing up, I never felt stable. I never felt like I was grounded and I never really felt safe. I felt like life was happening *to* me and that everyone around me was making choices for me I didn't want.

Subconsciously, I dealt with these feelings of insecurity by trying to control and micromanage my environment, as well as attempting to control what other people thought of me.

From the time I was a child, as young as age five, I was trying to control my environment. Each night before I went to bed, I'd arrange all my stuffed animals on the bed—each of them on a specific spot. I literally couldn't sleep until they were all perfectly placed in their designated position. I didn't have control of my life, which was obviously under the supervision of my family, so I tried to gain the control where I *did* have it, and at such a young age, that was in the placement of my stuffed toys.

This behavior of wanting to stay in control continued throughout my childhood, into adolescence and through to adulthood. As I got older it just shifted forms. It morphed from micromanaging my stuffed animals to trying to manage the behavior of others, thinking that if *they* could just do [BLANK] differently, then everything in *my* life would flow smoother. This would only cause me to complain and gossip about what others were doing, leaving me in a state of constant judgment and disapproval.

I also wanted to control other people's opinions of me. I wanted to be liked. What I now see as a lack of love and approval towards myself, manifested as trying to gain this love and approval from everyone else. This caused me to manipulate *who I was* in an effort to have others like me. I'd sacrifice being myself, using my voice and being open and honest about who I was. In reality, I didn't even take the time to get to know myself—I just put on the masks of what I thought other people wanted from me.

I tried to manipulate the men that came into my life, trying to convince them to love me when they weren't able to show it, not realizing at the time that by holding on so tight, I only pushed them further away.

Above that, I tried to *force* things to happen in my life before the timing was right, which only caused internal stress and tension.

For years and years, I held onto the images of what I *thought* my life was meant to look like and what I thought others would accept of me, all the while abandoning the person I really *felt* like on the inside. It was only in the *letting go* that I was able to discover and embody the woman I actually am. This wasn't someone I had to force and manipulate myself into being, rather, it was the person that shone through the moment I decided to stop trying to *control* who I was and what people thought about me.

We're going to talk about a couple different areas you need to address in your life:

1. **Control**
   - Letting go of controlling life
   - Letting go of controlling other people.

2. **Opinions**
   - Letting go of other people's opinions
   - Letting go of your own opinions.

Control

Letting go of controlling life

When we're operating in a state of Over Action it's really an attempt to gain control over our life circumstances. By being in control of our actions we're under the illusion that we're in control of our lives and what will transpire in the future. This, however, is just that... an *illusion*.

We're actually focusing control in all the wrong places. Real control isn't desperate and anxious. It's calm and peaceful. There are only certain areas of life we have any real control, and distinguishing what these areas are is important so we don't feel like we're running around aimlessly and anxiously.

All control of circumstances is an illusion of control. Control over our internal world is the only place we have a real say. This is good news yet some of you might take it as bad news. Don't worry. I initially thought this was bad news too, because I thought and felt I was good at controlling things outside of myself. I spent the first part of my life deluding myself into thinking I knew what was going on. I liked the tangible. Manipulating what I could see and touch felt more realistic than attempting to control my internal world.

Growing up I felt like I had no say whatsoever in what was going on in my life. Everything and everyone seemed to whisk me away in whatever direction most benefitted them, including and especially my parents.

Finally, after attempting to control everything outside of me with multiple failed attempts, I gave up on taking action and control over circumstances imposed upon me. I was over it. Over clinging to something I felt I couldn't change. I felt like I was giving up on life, but what I soon realized was that I was actually only giving up all the ways of living that no longer served me and was making way for new ones to come in that *did* serve me.

Letting go of the control of your outside world, circumstances, your body, and other people often feels like giving up, *especially* to your ego. If you're action orientated like I was, this can also feel like an internal death or a total failure of who you are and what you're doing.

Once I gave up on this need to control everything I suddenly gained a new feeling of being able to control something else—my thoughts and emotions. They were something no one else could touch. They were a part of a world that I, and only I, had access to. A gem I couldn't ignore—there when everything else around me seemed to be crumbling.

I know what you're probably thinking… but my outside world *is* what I want to change. The good news is that by changing your inside world of thoughts and feelings, you *are* in turn effecting change in your outside world, albeit in a more highly effective way!

A lot of teachers who have been mentors to me call this "surrendering." But the term "surrendering" never really resonated with me on a level I could understand it. Surrender felt like another thing I had to go out and do to "become" a better person or to "become" who and what I wanted to be.

When I started giving up, the Universe rushed in to help guide me through the areas of my life where I felt lost. It was like I could feel a strong presence waiting to bust the door down and, as soon as I created enough space by *letting go*, this force came in to rearrange those portions of my life I had previously attempted to micromanage.

You see I'd been arranging them in the way I thought they should be in accordance to who I wanted to be. But I didn't truthfully know exactly how those things should have been organized outside of myself because I wasn't being true to who I really was and, therefore, they weren't truly reflecting me. All I knew is how I wanted to *feel*. It was the moment I gave up trying to manipulate every detail in order to feel the way I wanted, the Universe was right by my side, thanking me for getting the hell out of my own way!

It was the Universe that knew how the details of my life should shift and rearrange to best suit the way I wanted to feel.

Again, I turn to my struggles with my body, fitness, and food as an example.

I'd look at pictures of perfect fitness models and athletes, and decide this was how I wanted my body to look. Then I figured what I needed next was a strict workout plan and the meticulous calculating and monitoring of what food I ate.

This helped me believe I was in control of my body and in control of how I looked. But something didn't feel right. As I've made super clear by now, I despise being told what to do and how to do it, so this strict plan made me want to rebel. It felt restrictive. I would stick to my diet and workouts one hundred percent until I did one tiny thing that wasn't in the plan. This one tiny thing would feel like a huge failure, leading me to completely binge on all the foods I couldn't eat on my plan. The foods that were just too high in calories for me to be eating regularly and still reach my fitness goals.

After stuffing anything and everything "bad" into my mouth and reaching the verge of throwing up *then* I'd feel like a *real* failure. I'd fall asleep in tears, vowing to myself, I'd be back on track and fully dedicated the next day.

The problem was this cycle repeated itself over and over again.

My breaking point came on Thanksgiving 2014 when a week before the holiday, I began spending hours scouring the internet and Pinterest, looking up and saving multiple dessert recipes I wanted to make. I was obsessive. I would literally be one picture away from drooling on my phone screen.

The day before Thanksgiving I woke up at the house of the guy I was seeing, and made a mad dash out to the grocery store so I could spend the day in the kitchen preparing for my binge the following day. I was so excited my heart raced.

I spent the *entire* day making pecan butter tarts, raisin butter tarts, cinnamon buns, sugar glazed pecans, gingersnap cookies and pumpkin pie. *All fucking day*! I literally didn't sit down until I collapsed into bed late that night. Of course, as I baked I started to taste the sweets. Before I knew it, I was in a near sugar coma.

The next day came and all I could think about was Thanksgiving dinner and the dessert feast to follow, vowing that because I messed up while I was baking the day before, I would eat healthy and "clean" until dinner that night. I also went to the gym and added an extra 30 minutes of cardio to my workout plan to make up for the previous night's feast, feeling deeply guilty and ashamed.

My frenzied thinking pattern felt like a sickness. Looking back on it now, I believe it was.

Dinner came and I stuffed myself. Then dessert came and I stuffed myself even more—to the point I involuntarily threw up. I ate so much my body literally couldn't fit it all in. Physically, I felt like garbage, but nothing could make up for the emotional pain I was feeling. I hated myself. I hated my behavior. I hated everything about how I felt and the subsequent thoughts that ran through my mind about how badly I was screwing up.

Worst of all, I could see the man I was dating hated it too. I could tell he was done. He barely looked at me and didn't touch me that evening. I felt grotesque and his reaction made me feel like he saw the same grossness within me.

I was failing. The things I was holding onto the strongest and trying to control were the very things that were slipping through my fingers.

How was this *happening*?

I made a decision the following morning to stop calculating my food. I felt like a baby taking her first steps.

Ironic, isn't it? This was the one area I was the most terrified of losing control over, yet I had *already* lost control. I learned that by letting go of my need to control, I actually gained more control than I ever had before, but just in a different way.

Even though I wanted the change to happen overnight, it took time. I had to feel my way into it by taking those baby steps.

I sit here a year later. Thanksgiving is next weekend. This time I feel a peace in my heart and a calmness knowing I made the right choice. I feel a pride in myself for being willing to learn, to change, and to grow. I've gained an understanding of what I had to go through and overcome to be where I am at right now.

I still over-indulge in sweets here and there, but not in the same way. Now when I eat these so-called "bad" foods, I don't look at them or myself as bad. They just are. They're neutral. I allow myself to eat what I want, when I want and, as a result, I eat more healthfully then I did when I was micromanaging my meals and feeling like one slip up made me a failure. I now see eating healthy and working on my fitness as an ever-changing journey that comes in waves and flows rather than something that's right or wrong, good or bad. It just is. It flows and changes as I do and I allow just that.

My workouts aren't something I have to check off my list of things to do each day, but something I choose to do to keep my body healthy. And when I don't have time or there's some other priority I would rather focus on, I don't obsess about it. I just let it go. Sometimes a few days go by and I don't work out at all and I'm okay with that.

I take each day as it comes, always honoring my body and my emotions. On some days I am simply too tired to work out. On other days my Divine feminine is screaming at me to just take a bath and have a solid cry or sleep in and get the extra rest. Other times, I take a day off and then come eight in the evening I feel the overwhelming urge to throw on some music and go for a run. I honor what my body needs when it needs it. Always checking in with myself—keeping myself motivated when I feel the inspiration slipping, but knowing when I need to stop pushing and take a break.

I monitor what I'm eating and how I'm treating my body based on how I feel when I eat different foods and how my body reacts to different exercises. I realized that I actually really enjoy going to the gym and lifting weights, but when it was something I was forcing myself to do because I feared getting fat, I started to hate it. When I'm honoring my body and myself, it's the main form of exercise I choose—at least at this stage in my life! I'm also open that this might very well change over time.

Life is ebb and flow. It's the ever-flowing cycle of energy. It's movement. And it sure as shit isn't about sticking to some rigid way of being, whether that's the diet plan you're following, or your school through to retirement *life* plan.

Happiness isn't found in following a strict plan. It's found through honoring each moment as it occurs, as well as each situation and person as they show up. It's the constant learning of how to tune into your own body and emotions to see what you need in that very moment. Sometimes that's a chocolate bar! And guess what?

That's okay.

Letting go of controlling other people

The single biggest course correction we can make in life is moving away from reacting to judgments with only more judgments, and condemning those who have opinions that aren't in alignment with ours. Aren't we living that which we are condemning by lashing out at the people who are negatively projecting towards us?

How do you propose we solve the problem by attacking it with the same energy we are being attacked with in the first place?

So many religions hate, kill and lash out at people who live differently than them—supposedly in the name of "love." These crusaders claim they're coming from a place of peace to murder anyone who isn't living the same kind of love. How the fuck do you explain that?

The most extreme example of this is in countries with the death penalty where it's law to kill someone who has killed another. I've a difficult time understanding how we are to solve the problems of murder and war by attacking it with more murder and war.

The flaw lies within our thinking not within the person we are attacking.

A couple of weeks ago in a neighboring town, someone broke into the house of a single father and his two-year-old daughter then killed him and kidnapped and ultimately murdered the little girl. This was absolutely horrible and the ripple effects of this double homicide could be felt throughout all of western Canada. The nation was traumatized.

As I scrolled through Facebook in the days following the murder, I read more words of hatred and anger than I did of compassion, love and grace. People publically posted and spoke out that the murderer should face death himself. He had taken and so he too should share the same fate.

I cringed when I read this because it exposed a flaw in the way our society thought... that we could solve the problem with the same energy that caused it in the first place. That we can use a particular behavior to manipulate a behavior within another. I'm in no way condoning what this man did. It makes me sick to my stomach, and my prayers go out to the two lives taken and the rest of their families, but I do under-stand that what ultimately caused the man to murder these two innocent souls was a sickness in his mind, his thoughts, and in the way he wanted to solve his problems. Yet aren't we using the same rationale if we sentence him to death?

When I read other people's opinions about sentenc-ing him to the death penalty, I see the same sickness within the murderer's mind as I do in the person wanting to send him to the executioner. The only difference is that this man followed through on his thoughts whereas these people only talked about it.

I see no difference, except in the brutality of the actual act, in the thinking of the murderer and the thinking of the person who believes he in turn should be murdered.

It's only through letting go of other people's actions and trying to heal them with love rather than coming at them with anger, hate and an attempt to control their lives that we can save ourselves. Be it the judgment of a murderer or the judgment of an overweight person, the underlying principal is fundamentally the same. If we let the thinking and mind sickness of these murderers control our reactions then we only perpetuate the sickness. We only amplify it.

We absolutely cannot control what another person chooses to do in this lifetime and, in attempting to do so, I believe things just continue to spiral more and more out of control. Instead, we can use the observation of what other people are doing to get even better clarity on how we want to live our lives and treat other people.

It's through our positive actions, thoughts, and reactions that we'll impact the world and inspire other people to take charge of their own lives in the same way. This is the method in which we can execute control and this is the method we can use to bring more harmony to both our individual lives and to the world at large.

If there's one thing I know for sure it's that I've no say over how people choose to conduct themselves in this world. Neither do you. But there's also something else I know for certain, and that's that only I can choose how I react to what other people say and do. Be it someone who I see every day or some person popping up in the news or in my work. I have a choice in how I choose to see them.

I'm aware the example of the murderer is extreme, but I want to get my point across strongly because it's this same theory that you can use towards the other people in your life whose behavior and actions you might be frustrated with. Maybe it's your parents, coworkers or friends. Maybe it's the person in line in front of you at the grocery store. Whomever it is, it's not your job to control them.

People at a different stage of their personal evolution than myself are going to do, say, and be whatever the heck they want to show up as in this world, and I cannot live my life attached to their choices and allow them to affect mine. They might choose to have an attachment to the things I do and say, and I have no control over this. I do, however, have control over whether I allow their opinions to affect me.

It takes a reversal in the way we've been thinking, acting, and reacting up until now. It takes a total undoing of everything we've known and a rebuilding of belief systems and thought processes from the ground up.

It all starts with deconstructing what you expect other people to do and say.

If we all became less concerned with what everyone else was doing and simply focused on the bettering of our lives and selves, it's my belief the world would become a lot more peaceful than it is now.

It's not our job to look at that which we don't accept in another and try to change it so it's more like us. It's our job to look within ourselves to see what's causing us discord, and make a choice to love that part or change and conduct ourselves in a way that makes us feel better. In the loving of that which we have previously rejected, we set ourselves free from that which is going on within everybody else's lives.

Those people who aren't like us aren't there for you to look at and then try to change. They're there to show you what you do and don't like within yourself. They're there to be the regulators of the qualities you're showing and bringing to the world. They're there to reflect something back to you. It's our relationship to others that shows us who we are.

Without someone or something to compare to we wouldn't know what we want at all or who we even are. Those who "trigger" us or make us feel discord in any way are oftentimes the ones to whom we need to pay most attention. We wouldn't feel this misalignment if there wasn't something presented that needed our attention.

Trying to control others is a powerless way of attempting to control our own lives. Stop looking in the wrong place and start looking in the place that empowers you and gives you your power back. By trying to control other people, you in turn are giving them the power to control you, which is the exact opposite of your intention.

Opinions

Letting go of other people's opinions

Aside from letting go of controlling how other people *behave*, letting go of other people's *opinions* will set us free even further.

This showed up in my life in the form of an old friendship. She was a very angry person. She made it known when anything didn't go the way she wanted it to or whenever someone acted in a way she thought they shouldn't. For years, I considered her to be one of my best friends. I was even a bridesmaid at her wedding.

For a long time, I was caught up in people pleasing, and thought I had to tweak who I was, what I did, and what I said to keep the peace between myself and everyone else. With such a controlling person as one of my best friends, this made things very taxing. She was quick to flip the switch from compassion to anger and while I watched her do it to other people, I always tried to avoid being the victim.

As I started making notable transformations in my life such as halting my drinking and partying and started focusing on what I really wanted, she became very disapproving. She would suddenly get defensive over her own drinking and social life while making subtle stabs at me and the way I was choosing to live.

On one level, I wanted to tell her to fuck off every time she offered up some snarky comment about my choices, but on another, I saw it from a bigger picture perspective. These altercations were testing me and also pushing me into clarifying and getting confident in understanding what kind of life I wanted for myself.

She would often question my choices, commenting, "Why do you have to be such a Debbie Downer? Can't you just come to the bar, have fun, and not drink?" When she'd say things like this to me initially, I thought she was right! Why *couldn't* I go out to the bar as usual with my friends and still have a good time?

You see my annoyance about her bringing up anything about my new lifestyle was really only a reflection of my insecurity about the choices I was making. It was a signal, as well as a sign, that I hadn't fully owned and committed to my truth. Choosing sobriety was about choosing truth—*my* truth.

If I had let her opinions about my lifestyle change get to my head and heart, which they threatened many times to do, then I probably wouldn't be living the life I'm living today. A life that feels so peaceful, joyful, ever expanding, and in complete alignment with my deepest truth.

I had to let her opinions go to move forward and continue making positive changes.

At first when this friend, or anyone else, would challenge my decisions to be sober and to remove myself from the bar scene, I'd react defensively. I'd come back at them with the same energy with which they came at me, and that response obviously only escalated the tension.

On one occasion this friend asked me whether I'd be okay dating someone who did occasionally go out to bars and drink, even if it was just for some wings and beers with the buddies. Initially, when she asked me this, I felt my stomach clench, and I began stammering. I knew I didn't want someone who did those things, but there was a part of me that didn't actually *believe* that such a man existed.

Instantly, she reflected this insecurity to me by essentially saying, "Good luck finding any guy who *doesn't* do this."

Over the next few years I realized there were, in fact, not *some*, but *many* men who didn't live their social life drinking at bars if even just to casually watch a game, and I've met a *ton* of them. Also, I understand that by her asking me this, I was being forced, or at least nudged, to clarify what I was actually looking for in a relationship. It forced me to commit to what I really wanted. It forced me to speak my desires out loud.

This particular friend continued to offer up opinions about my life, what I was doing, and boundaries I was setting with her and others. Less than a year after standing at the altar at her wedding ceremony, we don't speak at all.

The only difference between all the other times and this time is that I didn't run and try to mend things for the sake of her not being mad at me. Instead, I took a hard look at how I was showing up in this friendship and in the world, and checked to see if I was honoring myself. I realized that throughout the majority of my friendship with her, I wasn't.

I've speculated a hundred times about what she must think of me now. There would be an endless litany of judgments and disapproving remarks about my life choices. But then I remember that had this person really been a friend she wouldn't have disappeared from my life at the time I started to step into my truth. Instead she'd have supported my transformation. I had to let go of her judgments towards me, as well as my choices, even if that meant losing the friendship.

Over the past few months, I've done a lot of writing and forgiveness work in letting go of the judgments I think she might have developed towards me. I've also done a lot of work on letting go of the judgments I have towards her, as well as how she conducted herself in the friendship and within the diminishing and eventual death of it. The truth is that even if I forgive her and myself for how everything worked out, if I still hold onto her opinions of me and mine of her, she has power over me. And I want no one having power over me but myself!

So I choose to let it go. There's nothing I need to "do" per se, but set the intention to free myself. As a consequence, each time this issue comes up for me, which it has more than once, I make the conscious effort to let it go. In the process, I gave up the notion she is the person my ego wants to blame, as well as the idea I've done wrong by not running to please her and to be willing to let the friendship go. I've also accepted that who I am isn't dependent upon what someone else thinks of me, no matter how negative the thought or how many people back that person up.

This doesn't mean I'm perfect or that I always make the "right" decision. It just means I pay more attention to the subtleties along the way nudging me from the inside to do what will serve me best. Now when I get off track, I spend *less* time off track than I used to before steering myself back on course.

It means that whenever someone hates or judges me for what I've supposedly done wrong or that they don't like from their perspective I don't allow it to veer me as far off course as I did in the past.

As I mentioned in the previous section and that particular scenario with my friend, it wasn't just important for me to let go of what her opinions towards me were, but to also let go of the opinions and judgments I had towards *her*. Just like her opinions of me don't define me, nor do my opinions about her and how she conducted herself in this situation, define her. This is important to recognize.

Part of me wanted to point the finger at her, blame and punish, but my Higher Self wanted to let all that shit go. I wanted to allow her the space to be who she chooses to be while also putting my energy into being who I want to be.

It's your job to show up as yourself. Then, by honoring your self-truth, you can trust that the right people will show up to support you. By forcing your opinion on others you actually do the opposite and attract what you don't want into your life.

Even the supposed "positive" things become detrimental to your relationships when forced upon another. Veganism is a perfect example. I see more hostile and angry vegans online than I do peaceful ones. You can't defend the peace and joy of an animal while verbally and physically attacking another human. That's the most hypocritical thing I've come across yet I see it all the time.

A couple of years ago, I joined a "Vegan Bodybuilding" group on Facebook when I was struggling with the amount of protein my trainer was telling me I needed in a day. I was having a difficult time getting it into my diet without eating meat. I thought vegan bodybuilding would be the place to find the answers on how to live a plant-based lifestyle while also living a fit life.

I couldn't have been more wrong. While there were many useful tidbits on how to eat plant-based food to build muscle, mostly what I saw was a cult-like grouping that excluded everyone who wasn't following their philosophy a hundred percent of the time.

People would post anecdotes about their journey, maybe saying they had cut out meat but were still struggling with dairy and eggs only to have every angry vegan on the page personally attack them—name calling and all.

These newbies were showing up and trying hard to make a change and a difference to their health, as well as the wellbeing of animals only to be bombarded with hostility for not doing it the "perfect" way as defined by the rest of the group. And this is the thinking that's supposed to save our world, our animals, and our planet? This is the treatment our fellow human beings receive when they want to create a world of peace and love?

I don't think so.

Peace comes from an acceptance of all. It comes from dropping judgments against others and yourself via a process of letting go of other people's judgments towards yourself, no matter how deep the initial sting.

During this time, in order to reach my protein goal, I was also eating a lot of eggs and dairy products to make up for the lack of meat in my diet. When I would be on this Facebook page, I'd start harshly judging not just the angry people lashing out, but also myself for not following the proposed strictly vegan diet.

Peace comes from a celebration of what our fellow humans and *we* are doing right rather than shitting all over them for what they're apparently doing wrong, according to your criteria. That's what creates lasting change. That's what lifts people up, and encourages them to be happier and kinder and more joyful.

We *all* deserve the same love, understanding, and acceptance. And it's through the demonstration of this love and compassion to those people, regardless of the choices, no matter how poor or hurtful, that'll in turn teach those exact same people to carry out the same acts of love in their own life. It's this same love and compassion we aim to demonstrate towards others, that we must also demonstrate towards *ourselves*, letting go of the judgments we place both towards other people and towards ourselves.

There's someone in your life who puts more pressure on you than any other individual and group of people in the world combined. This person has an image and idea of what you should be and will stop at nothing from beating you up to become this.

This person is **YOU**.

Letting go of your own opinions

At the end of the day, beyond all other opinions and expectations, that which matters most is only your internal world. What you think of yourself. How you feel about yourself. The actions you choose to take and *why*.

During my early life I grew up with an ideal image in my head of who I "should" be. This included what I should look like, how I should dress, what I should do for a living, who I should date, where I should hang out, who my friends should be, you name it...

Many choices I made came from the place of how I thought I should appear to everyone else and what image I wanted to portray. By the time I hit twenty-six, I realized I had such a long list of "should be's" and "should do's," that I physically didn't have enough hours in the day to do and be everything I had mentally listed.

When I entered the personal-growth profession and began coaching clients, I began researching how other coaches and writers ran their businesses and what philosophies they espoused. Many of these approaches were similar to one another, so I thought I needed to do things a certain way. I automatically put it on myself that I had to do the same things and show up in the same way as those successful people. This was a lot to put on myself. And besides that, I felt a yucky feeling within the pit of my stomach whenever I examined what someone else was doing and assumed that to be successful or feel good I'd have to go about it in the same way. I very quickly tuned into this feeling and modified my old behavior of trying to alter who I was by taking on the role of a student. I subsequently was able to learn what they were doing and implement only what resonated with me into my own life and business in a way that suited me. This might seem like a subtle shift, but I assure you it was a big shift indeed.

The truth of the matter is, no one has to tell me what I have to do, or when, why, or how. All I have to do is simply look within and around myself, observe, extrapolate and from *there* conclude how I need to show up as a unique individual with a story and message to share and then make myself accountable to my own intention and set of success criteria.

After my breakup and downward spiral, I started working out and taking my health seriously. I began this part of my journey by looking at what fitness gurus and athletes were doing. I then placed massive pressure on myself to live up to the same standard. In my mind, to fit into the category of people who were fit, healthy and had nice bodies, I had to adopt the exact same lifestyle as them. Yet, as I implemented these oftentimes extreme lifestyle practices, every cell in my body screamed this didn't *feel* right for me. I continued to plow on regardless of the messages and the wisdom I was receiving, and continued operating within a health system that didn't resonate with who I was or am.

As mentioned previously, after over a year of meticulously calculating every morsel of food that passed my lips and micromanaging each hour of the day to fit in my two plus hour workouts in addition to many more hours spent on food preparation, I was at a breaking point. I wanted to say fuck it all and throw it all down the drain.

I had placed a massive *expectation* on myself to be something I wasn't, and to fit into an ideal image of what healthy fitness-minded people looked like and how they spent their time. In the process, I abandoned who I really was for the closed box minded image of who I thought I should be.

What I really wanted was to be healthy, fit, and flexible not just in my physical body, but also in my entire life, as well as in my time management. I didn't really want to live the lifestyle of a fitness or bikini model. It was too fucking exhausting. I realized I would rather put my energy into things that lit my heart up. I wanted to feel an expansive energy where I felt healthy, happy, and strong. This didn't translate into developing a six-pack and starving my body into submission by burning up every fat cell in it.

So I began asking myself questions...

Could I be someone who valued my life by taking care of myself physically, mentally, and emotionally according to my own criteria? Could I set my own guidelines about what was healthy and appropriate for my own body, even if that fluctuated from day to day? Could I set up my own system in accordance with what my intuition was telling me, and only accept information from the professionals that resonated with me and worked for my body? Could I be happy, healthy, and strong in my own body without looking like a bikini model?

The answer was **fuck yes**!!! That's exactly what I could do. But first I had to ditch the rules I'd made up of what I *should* do.

This same principle can be applied to all areas of your life and every decision you make.

In my twenty-sixth year I started questioning *everything* on a deeper level than I had done before. Prior to that I had listened to others about what I needed to do to move forward with my life, but then resisted all the advice they gave me. Now, I was getting down to the nitty-gritty. I began questioning my belief system, as well as the self-imposed "shoulds" to do with my job, my nutrition and exercise, the people I chose to spend time with, my living circumstances, and the way I spent every waking hour of every day.

In those moments, I chose to take personal responsibility for every aspect of my life that looked the way it looked, including every part I hated and every part I loved. No one was going to make decisions for me anymore or tell me what I had to wake up and do every morning except for that little voice in my heart.

Freedom ensued.

Freedom from the prison walls I had built around myself. Freedom from the schedule I told myself I had to meticulously follow. Freedom from what every person in my life expected of me, as well as freedom from their constant demands.

I was living for me now. Not for who I thought I should be, but for who I was and am. I didn't need to *find* or *uncover* this person. All I needed to do was to drop the expectations of others, and follow what that little voice inside had been whispering for years and which had now blossomed into true authenticity, grace and genuine strength.

Internal vs. External

When trying to create permanent transformation, the change must occur first on an internal level. This is the most *efficient* and *maintainable* way to create change. Yet, most of the time we are taught to make the change on an external level, *forcing* and pushing for the outside result we desire. In reality, the external circumstances of our life are a reflection of our internal world, meaning that when we make a change on this internal level, our outside circumstances will mold and shift accordingly to match up with this change.

Another way to view this would be to see our outside life circumstances as a symptom, not the true ailment. Rather than trying to heal the symptom at the level of the symptom, we create change most effectively by healing on the level of what's *causing* the symptom—in this case it's our internal world. When I speak of our internal world, I'm talking about the world that goes on inside of yourself. The part of you that no one else can really see with their eyes, but that you can very clearly feel and *know*. It's the part of yourself that no one but you can possibly know. It's the world of your thoughts, feelings, beliefs, expectations, and assumptions. It is that part of our world that, in my opinion and experiences, is largely ignored by modern western society. Yet, it's the part we should focus on the *most* if we're to create a life we love and that's in alignment with our deepest desires.

Pushing and manipulating for a particular outcome can leave us feeling nothing but frustration and powerlessness. Oftentimes, it comes with a lot more exerted effort than an attempt to make change on the level of where it can be sustained.

The Law of Attraction teaches us that like is drawn towards like—not just on the physical planes, but also on the *energetic* planes. The Law of Attraction is what's causing our internal world to attract *like* things that manifest as our outside circumstances. With this law in mind, it can be explained why lasting and sustainable change happens through manipulating our inside world rather than the struggle to manipulate our outside world.

This can be so clearly exemplified through romantic relationships, where it seems to be the one most accepted environment in our society to manipulate another person. Think about it... we look towards our partner to provide us with a certain feeling and to *fill* us up emotionally. This is what almost every Disney and Hollywood romance movie portrays. The protagonist is invariably a single, struggling, and sad bachelorette whose life is empty and meaningless until a hero comes along, saves her, and fills her up with all the loving emotions she was previously missing.

This story line screws up our expectation of real life relationships because it causes us to look toward our partner as the source of our happiness and fulfilled emotions. Then, when we aren't getting these needs met by our partner, which they can't possibly consistently provide us with because they're human and are going to have their bad days too, we feel empty and think something's *missing*. In a desperate attempt to be filled back up with these missing emotions, we often look towards that person and try to force *them* to change and meet our needs.

In this example, we're trying to get our emotional needs met by manipulating the outside circumstances rather than tweaking our inside world to allow for the outside manifestations of that shift to show up. This might be a whole new way of looking at things that you've never been introduced to before, but I want you to keep an open mind because it has been the very implementation of these ideas into my life that I've created and continue to sustain *massive* transformation and fulfillment.

Once your internal environment is changed, the law of attraction will naturally draw a matching effect to it. Let's talk about the example of a romantic relationship. When your partner is having a bad day and not feeling or acting loving and joyful, most people's initial reaction is to feel shut down or even hurt especially if they've been looking towards this person to fill their emotional cup. A typical reaction could be to get defensive towards that person or trying to push them into being in a better mood, or even getting mad at them for their bad mood. I've seen and *done* this is my past relationships. It transpired into me shutting down emotionally, lashing out at my partner, and getting mad at him for being seemingly cold towards me. The truth is, if someone is having a difficult day, it can be hard enough for them to keep their own energy up without having to also try and keep their partner's up as well.

Instead of reacting in a way that attempts to manipulate the person into a good mood, we can use the idea of creating internal change to experience the outside circumstance we desire. I had such a situation happen recently when the man I was dating was in a less than happy mood. He wasn't taking it out on me, but I sensed it right away, even through his text messages. He just seemed a little *off*—not overly chatty and rather consumed with his thoughts.

My initial reaction when I sensed this energy from him was to put my defenses up and push him away because he wasn't being attentive to me in his usual manner. However, having the awareness that I now do, I stopped myself and consciously took a moment to change my perspective.

He was in a down mood and this had nothing to do with me. I knew that I rely on myself to fill myself up emotionally and emanate love rather than expecting him to be my source of love, so I asked myself how I could be this idea *in action*. Rather than defaulting to my old way of reacting by pushing him away or even causing an argument, I acted *towards* him with love.

We met at the gym together for a workout that afternoon where we'd usually train together. It was obvious that he wanted to plug in his ear buds and have a workout of his own. Instead of feeling hurt or offended by this, I understood this was his way of dealing with his bad mood. I kissed him and told him that it was okay to have days like this. He didn't need to be fixed—he was human like all of us and would experience fluctuating emotions on any given day.

The key here is that I didn't allow his negative mood to bring my own down. I simply gave him space and chose to maintain my own feelings of happiness, love and elation. We both went on to complete our workouts. He later thanked me for being so understanding, and I noticed how much better he seemed to be feeling by the time we were finished.

You see, rather than trying to manipulate my outside circumstances in this situation such as his mood and behavior, I simply chose to control my own internal environment by holding myself in a loving, compassionate, and understanding energy. This, in turn, without my even trying, brought that same love, compassion, and understanding feelings back to me.

This is just one example of a time where we can choose to have awareness and control over our internal world so that we can experience the outside circumstances we desire, without forcing them. The results we want never come from manipulating or trying to control another person's behavior or mood.

Another example of creating change in this way can be articulated through health and fitness. The fitness industry *thrives* and *survives* on luring you into making change on an external level only, which as we talked about before it *doesn't really* work long term, nor does it feel harmonious. It continuously sends the message that if you manipulate your body and what you put into it in just the right way (everybody's "right" way is seemingly different too) *then* you will have the body you want.

While there's some truth to this, of course, it isn't the *easiest* way. It's actually the most *difficult* way! And that's also why so many people struggle to create sustainable change on this level.

Creating change internally in terms of body composition, diet, and exercising looks more like creating an environment of love from the inside out. Spending time paying attention to your body, how it feels, what it needs, and how it reacts to what you put in it and do with it. Creating long-term change isn't about placing unrealistic and torturous expectations and limitations on yourself. Change on this level would comprise of an ongoing expression of self-love towards your core self and your body by changing your internal dialogue from one of self-hatred to one of self-love.

Instigating change and transformation from this level creates a space from which inspiration to treat your body better, as well as nourish and exercise it, is born. This is the place to take action from—not from the place of torturing yourself into an ideal of what you think you *should* be doing.

Earlier this week I came across an article written by Jon Gabriel, creator of "The Gabriel Method" that encourages weight loss and healthy living through the power of healing the mind rather than manipulating the body only. One of the biggest factors, according to Jon, in his two hundred and twenty pound weight loss, was that he refused to control what he ate. No foods were off limits and if he craved something, he allowed himself to have it.

Now, this pretty much goes against every "health" and weight loss tip most of us have ever been given. We're constantly bombarded with information on which foods are "good" and "bad," as well as what we need to avoid at all costs and what we can indulge in on occasion. This translates into a strict set of rules intended to control our lives.

By dropping the control and *letting go*, Jon was able to go from morbidly obese to muscular, fit, and healthy in a matter of two and a half years. This was the effect of merely letting go and taking conscious control over his internal environment thus translating into action taken and noticeable change in his external environment.

Of course, some amount of change can happen by forcing your body to do what it doesn't want to do, but this doesn't last and it sure doesn't feel as good. When focusing on a healthy mindset around health, rather than forcing your approach, it's the Inspired Action to exercise and to treat your body well that manifests into results.

When we can release our desperate need to manipulate and control our lives, other people, and situations into what we think they should be, we can begin to take responsibility for the environment we're creating in our minds, take charge *there*, and create change towards the life we've been dreaming about and longing to attain. Once we surrender that which we feel has been running the show then it loses its power. It's only when you try to micromanage these areas that they seem to be the ones calling the shots.

Self Reflection Exercises

A large part of letting go is taking our attention *off* that which we don't want and *towards* what we do want. In this exercise, I want you to focus on the very real yet virtual world of social media where any and all information is available to us at the touch of a button or the swipe of a screen. All of this technology and networking tools are truly beautiful, but they require conscious effort. Only focus your attention on that which does you the greatest good.

- Go through your Facebook friends list and unfriend or unfollow every person whose story you come across that doesn't inspire you or make you feel good. At the time of writing this book, Facebook has introduced an awesome feature where you can unfollow someone without actually unfriending them. This means you don't have to see what they post on their feed without them knowing and that they can still see your feed!

- Go through your Instagram and Snapchat and any other social media accounts you use, and unfollow anybody that does not elevate your energy or inspire you.

By doing this, you're choosing what you look at and focus on while simultaneously letting go of the negativity that lowers your own energy.

Chapter 13:

Layer 6 – Embodiment

Knowledge without implementation is basically useless. Just *knowing* a theory isn't enough. We *must* implement the information we learn in order to better our lives.

I was chuckling at myself the other day as I was telling someone I used to read all these spiritual books at the same time I was out partying every weekend, drinking and doing drugs! I would read the material and feel a deep sense of resonance and understanding, but the life I was actually living was not reflecting the insights I was absorbing. This is because I kept the information I was reading and learning at an intellectual level, instead of taking the ideas and applying them to my life. The information and insights, therefore, remained nothing more than entertainment. It wasn't until I took action to make changes that my life started to reflect these spiritual truths.

Simply *knowing* something *isn't enough!!!*

Here, I want to talk to you about embodiment, which is to *become* the expression of the things you wish were more present in your life. That which you desire ties directly into what we just talked about in regard to creating change on an internal level. When we become the expression of the aspects we want *more* of in our life, the Law of Attraction must bring more of those aspects into our life. So, rather than going to the outside and looking for the feelings we wish to fill up on, we want to become the generator of those very feelings!

An Inclusion Based Universe

There's a law that currently governs what's going on in your life whether you know it or not. So understanding and using it consciously will make your life more harmonious, joyful, and flow with grace and ease. Things you used to labor to attract now seamlessly show up on your doorstep, and struggle becomes a thing of the past.

This law is as true and real as gravity. It's working all the time whether you have an awareness of it or not, but *having* an awareness of it allows you to use it in your favor to create the feelings and circumstances in your life that are desirable. This law says we live in an Inclusion Based Universe.

What does an Inclusion Based Universe *mean*?

It means we can't exclude something from our life by focusing on it and trying to force it to go away. The fact we're focusing on it means it's inherently included in our life. The Universe doesn't recognize whether you're keeping your attention on something because you love it or hate it, or whether you desire its presence or desire its departure. It reads only that your attention *is* on whatever it's on, and thus *includes* this in your life.

Where this principle can go rather sideways in our life is when we experience something we *don't* want and instead of then looking for its opposite by establishing what we *do* want, we look at the thing we don't want and shout at it to GO AWAY! But what happens is that by looking at it and declaring we don't want to experience it is that we continue to attract more of it into our lives. This declaration can happen through our actual words or simply through our thoughts. The Universe only hears that you're thinking about and focusing your attention in this area and so more of the same is included in your life.

When I first learned this principle, it actually scared me because the only way I knew how to deal with my life was by looking around, seeing what I hated about the way I was living, and then attempting to *push* those things out, as is the case with *so many* people. I didn't even know I was doing this—it was just the way my brain was programed to process my world and what was happening in it.

This isn't just occurring on a personal level, but on a societal and global one too. The western world is currently participating in a war against terrorism yet there are more terrorist attacks taking place than ever before. There's a war against drugs yet more people are dying from drug use and overdoses than ever before. There's a war against every group of people you could possibly imagine. No matter who they are and what they stand for, there seems to be someone fighting a war against them.

There are actually wars occurring in the name of peace! For fuck's sake, how does *that* make any sense?

Nothing can be fought out of our lives. It's not the solution.

The solution is **inclusion,** where attention is drawn away from the issues at hand and we begin focusing on what we want to be included in our personal lives and as a society, country, and planet.

Instead of fighting against the terrorists we could be supporting peace groups. We could be spreading love to countries that need our help instead of waltzing in and killing them. Instead of getting all up in arms and complaining when the Starbucks attendant gets our order wrong, we could choose to take a different perspective and say to ourselves that maybe that person was having a bad day and maybe we can cheer them up by being kind to them. This brings kindness, which we *want* to include, to the situation, rather than focusing on the mistake and the annoyance we feel because of it.

We can only invite what we want into our life by focusing on the aspects we do want rather than pushing against the aspects that we do not want.

The negatives are here for a reason. They're here to show us what we need to focus on. They're showing us areas of our life that are in misalignment with our greater good. I believe life shakes us up to get our attention pointed in a direction we weren't previously looking in and indeed need to orient ourselves. Sometimes this shakeup comes in the form of an injury, illness, breakup, or even an "accidental" breakdown of a phone or computer or other piece of technology. These incidents grab our attention. They manifest out of a need for us to focus on something in particular and to steer our life in a specific direction—not to push back in resistance and retaliation.

Just the other day this happened in my brother's life. He'd been having dental issues for over a year. He was going back and forth between different dentists—none of whom were able to target the exact problem or where it was occurring. After a few fillings and a few root canals, he thought the issue had finally been resolved, but was then told by another dentist he needed yet another root canal.

He phoned me in a panic to get a hold of our mom whom he'd called numerous times and who wasn't answering. The dentist had hit something in my brother's jaw. It had ruptured and his mouth began filling with fluid. The dentist immediately sent him to the hospital to meet up with an infection specialist who ordered a CT scan. Without waiting for the results, the doctor began expressing his concern, and said there could potentially be vascular tumors, cancerous or benign, dwelling in my brother's jaw.

It took several days to get the results. During the time my brother waited he filled his mind with worry, panic and the negative anticipation that his worst-case scenario had manifested into a reality.

He described to me what he would do if, in fact, it was a cancerous tumor. He didn't want treatment. He wanted to just move to the mountains and live out the rest of his life in the wilderness being one with nature.

The CT scans came back negative. There was no cancer and no tumor. It was a bad infection that was subsequently treated with a heavy dose of antibiotics. We all felt relieved and thankful!

This was Joe's wake-up call to pay attention to areas of his life that he was ignoring. It was a call to action for him to reevaluate how he was spending his time, with whom, and to let go of anything that brought him anything less than *joy*. So often we get caught up living the life we feel we have to while putting the things we love on the back burner.

If he loved living in the wilderness and being one with nature then why wasn't he doing that more often? Just because he wasn't diagnosed with cancer didn't mean that suddenly he had become immortal. Death could come to him tomorrow or in 80 years. Who knows! None of us do, and that's why it's important we implement the things we want *more* of in our life *right now!*

Yet here we are living as if we have forever... as if we have some control over when and where our bodies will make their exit. Do you think any person that has ever lived and is ever going to live on Earth knew or will know when they were going to die, with the obvious exception of suicides? Nobody wakes up and expects or plans to get into a fatal car accident that day. No one decides, "Oh, I think today I'll develop cancer and spend the rest of my days sick in bed." Nobody decides this! At least, not on a conscious level.

It so happens I believe we do choose our exit from our physical body and our physical world, but the choice is made from a soul perspective before we even enter into this earthly domain

The only agenda our life is following is the agenda of our soul, and its growth and expansion. It's not the agenda of the conscious mind or our ego in this body. Your body wants to live forever. Your ego wants to live forever. It feels threatened by the very conversation we're having right now because it wants to persuade you otherwise. It has spent your entire life convincing you of its truth. Most people you know are also operating within the manipulative realm of their respective egos.

This isn't truth. Life's temporary. It's precious. It needs to be lived NOW before the accident that immobilizes you or a cancer shows up to tell you that you aren't living the joy that is your birthright.

When dis-ease or injury show up to guide you in a different direction, listen and act and move towards what you want in this life. Move towards how you want to feel. That is what the ailment is showing you to do. It's here as a guide.

We've been conditioned to *fight* these things when they show up—to make them go away and to do absolutely everything in our power to kill them off. What if their presence isn't about killing them off? What if it's about looking at them exactly as they are, accepting they're here in this moment, and thanking them for showing us what needs our attention in our lives? Then, we can move into a place of peace and a place of healing our mind and body.

Every dis-ease starts as a dis-ease of the mind in the way our thinking interprets the events and people around us. We are deciphering them through the eyes of our ego rather than through the eyes of God or Spirit and the journey of our soul. This is the fundamental error. It's what causes suffering in this life and what makes us perceive our circumstances and who we are in a distorted and fractured way.

Being It

Now that I've made clear what inclusion is and how it governs our lives, we can now make better sense of embodiment and how to make it an active part of our reality.

As I've mentioned earlier, when we look at someone and feel either envious or inspired by them what we're really noticing are these qualities within *ourselves*. Feelings of jealousy or inspiration are life's way of getting our attention to these aspects and showing us that they want to be expressed *by* us too!

We have an innate ability to ignore those things that we already are and that are already in full expression within us, because we just simply *are* them. That which is itself can't analyze itself and see itself, and so that's why life provides us with the impeccable system of seeing our own qualities in another, thus being a mirror of ourselves. Truly brilliant if you ask me!

When people tell me they're inspired by me, and that they find my writing and sharing to be motivational, I don't see it. I'm happy to help invoke this feeling within someone through my creative work, but I don't see it. I don't inspire myself. I don't see it the way they do. Because I just am it. I'm being it without even thinking about it.

The fact that someone can find me inspiring means they resonate with what I'm saying. They resonate with the message, but they're not *fully* living and expressing it. The inspiration is leading them in the right direction, showing them what they would really desire to become, but it's also there to show them that they're not currently living what they want to be living. The inspiration is what's bridging the gap between who they are and who they want to be. Inspiration is pointing us in the direction of who we really are. Embodiment is the expression of this inspiration.

Beautiful, isn't it? Life has provided us with a whole set of tools and they're operational all the time. The problem has been that no one really showed or told us how to use them consciously to rocket fire our life into what we desire it to be.

Well, I am here to do just that!

I want to give you some perspective here because I know this probably sounds far out of reach from anything you've heard described to you before. In fact, it's probably the complete opposite of that which you've ever been taught. Stay with me.

Think of someone who's doing something great in the world. They're successful. They appear to be living their dreams. This might be someone in the public eye or someone you know personally. It might be a member of your family or it might be a famous singer, actor, or an athlete. Think of someone who's doing amazing things in the world, but doesn't *personally* inspire you.

They might be sports players, for example. I can see who they are on television yet I literally have no reaction. I feel no emotional reaction to what they've accomplished. I see they're successful, but I'm not moved in any way, shape, or form, by their profession. I also feel this way about western medical professionals, doctors, surgeons, and the like. The prestige they experience after years and years of schooling and the consequential higher than average income doesn't inspire me. While the accomplishment of finishing so much schooling might really ignite a spark in someone else's insides, I feel nothing. This is neither good nor bad—it just *is*.

Now, think about someone that really inspires you. Someone who, when you think about their life, who they are and what they do, really lights you up! It gets you excited and wanting to converse. You get goose bumps when you think about this person, and could literally close your eyes and envision yourself living the same type of life.

These people for me are authors, teachers, singers, dancers, and speakers of truth. They're the people who continually work on their self-growth and development while boldly expressing themselves. They're the people living their deepest and fullest expression because it's in them to live, not waiting for the world to give them permission or approval. They're the creatives of this world—the dancers, writers, speakers and teachers. I admire their work, and feel lit up and inspired when observing them.

Through my lifetime I idolized various figures in the world of personal development. I wanted to be like them. Admiration was at the forefront of my mind when I would read their books or listen to their lectures. When they described the joy and happiness they had created for themselves, I would squeal, "Yes, yes, YES!"

These inspirational people are usually the powerful women living out and speaking out their truth. They can be celebrities, but they can also be the girl who walks down the street fully expressing her personal fashion sense and not giving a fuck what anyone else thinks about her. I've always admired those people who don't care what other people think about them. They don't overstate their personal philosophy, exclaiming how they just don't give a fuck. For me that's clearly a deep rooted seat of insecurity behind the disguise of not caring. Rather, they're just living the life of who they want to be. They're busy tending to matters of their heart, nurturing themselves and their creative projects. They're too caught up in the love of building a life they desire to even notice the people who don't like them.

I've also always been somewhat enamored with fame and those people who are in the public eye. I've observed their lifestyle in awe, and secretly wished I could be rich and famous too. Previously when talking about such things, I'd feel shame wash over me, leaving me with a feeling that it was somehow *wrong* to desire fame and riches. Now I'm more comfortable owning my desires. Upon recognizing this, I realized that not everybody wants the same thing! At first, I couldn't fathom how someone *wouldn't* want to be rich, famous, and in the public eye. But now, I understand and realize that I'm fascinated with this because it's an aspect of myself that wants to be expressed through my creative projects. I want to be a famous author and speaker and *that*'s why fame and being in the public eye has always caught my interest and attention.

Ahhh... Such a *beautiful* thing!

So the reason I feel uninspired by athletes and surgeons is because they don't represent the qualities in me. However, I respect what they do in the knowing that others find them inspiring. I'm just not one of them. This isn't who I am, nor do I care to waste my precious time developing attributes in myself that don't light me up.

Instead, as mentioned previously, I feel overly inspired, goose bumpy, and smiley amongst the people doing activist work, and speaking their minds and hearts, and presenting contrarian views to popular opinion. Those people who give selflessly to others. Those people who are *creating*, birthing things into the world that weren't there before. The authors. The speakers. Those who can stand on stage and calmly share their lives with others, helping them navigate through their individual struggles.

Empowered women inspire me—the women living their truth, who harness their sexuality and love their bodies. This fucking lights me up!!!

Because this is who *I am*. These women represent qualities I want to embody even *more* of in my own life. They're aspects within myself, wanting to be expressed in greater ways than they already are.

I now look at people I admire and am inspired to see what qualities they are expressing that I clearly am denying or not fully nurturing in my own life. But it was not always like this. There was a time not long ago when I looked at the exact same people and felt sadness and resentment that they had achieved what I wanted while I fell short. It made me mad that some people were just apparently handed things in life while I struggled. I would say nasty things about them for living the life they did. In fact, what I was really doing in the guise of these insults was secretly wishing I could be living the same way. At the time I couldn't articulate it as such, but the deeper I analyze and observe myself, the further clarity I get.

This is an attitude from my past—an attitude I lived with for the first twenty plus years of my life. I see many others living by the same creed and it just requires a reversal of thinking to turn this seemingly negative quality into a positive one!

Embodiment isn't only the cultivation of the qualities you admire within another, but the living out of those qualities within your own life.

If you want more love in your life, show more love to people. Bring love to every project you create and every bill you pay. If you want more peace in the world, be more peaceful in situations that stress you out. Calm your mind in the face of stress. Breathe when you are stuck in traffic and enjoy the time of doing *nothing*, rather than cursing, stressing, and being angry. The drive is going to take you the same amount of time regardless, so you might as well feel at peace on the route!

You will experience what you put out into the world tenfold. It feels pretty good to appreciate the cashier at the grocery store, but you may feel challenged by showing appreciation for the boss or co-worker who's driving you up the wall. I would suggest showing the latter person some serious TLC and appreciation. When you can show this to the people that really trigger and frustrate you, your life will unfold in a whole new way that you've never experienced before.

This one took a long time for me to come to terms with and really accept as truth. I'd struggled with the same employer over and over again at every job—they just manifested in a different body. I could change salons or change industries all together and I assure you I would have attracted the same boss in a new setting.

I always felt underappreciated and overworked in every job I ever had.

Just recently, I had to sit down with my boss at the hair salon and have an uncomfortable conversation with her about taking more time off during the year than contracted. I knew this was an ongoing issue for most of the girls at work, so I was nervous about this conversation.

I asked her to stay late one night after the salon had closed and everyone had gone home. Shakily, I explained my situation to her and what I wanted to do. As stylists, we were allowed one month of vacation time per year, which translates into twenty working days off. I had already taken a week off, had booked to travel to Peru for another two weeks, and was now asking for another three to travel to Bali and Thailand.

What my boss didn't know was that I had already committed to the Bali trip before asking her permission. I had paid almost twenty thousand dollars to enroll in a mastermind coaching program, which included the journey in Bali. Ten days after returning from Peru, I would need to leave again until just a couple days before Christmas, which was our busiest time of the year. Faith was in the driver's seat at this point!

She told me I wouldn't be able to take more than the allowed four weeks off, and that maybe I could look into shortening one of my trips to make it work.

I was unwilling to accept this as my reality, and immediately put my problem-solving cap on. The light bulb switched on.

Since it was so close to the end of one year and the beginning of the next, what if I suggested I take vacation time from the upcoming year?

She was open to this suggestion, but urged me to think if I would be able to handle less than two weeks off the following year. While it wasn't my ideal situation, it was a sacrifice I was willing to make in order to make these trips a reality.

Amazing! We agreed that we could add up all my days off and see how many went over the four allowed weeks, and then sign a contract stating that I would take those days from the following year. This ensured that everything was fair and equitable for all staff.

Overwhelmed with gratitude and wanting to heal my ongoing issues with employers, shortly after that conversation with my boss I sat down at home and wrote her a letter. In it I expressed my gratitude and appreciation for everything she had done for me as a boss and as a person. I went on to say how appreciative I was for her making this exception for the time I wanted off, and that I know she was doing what she could to keep things fair for all the girls in the salon while still keeping us all happy and satisfied with our careers.

She texted me the night after I had given her the letter, saying it made her tear up and then proceeded to thank me for such a thoughtful letter. I felt my heart grow warm. It was a difficult letter to write because we had butted heads during our time working together, but I felt good about it.

A few months passed and one day at the salon, my boss pulled me aside and asked to speak to me in private. My heart pounded and my palms sweated. What did she want to talk about?

We stepped into the aesthetics room, closed the door and sat down. She proceeded to inform me she wasn't going to strip time away from the following year's vacation, but was allowing me to take the full time I needed for the trips I had planned. It was something she had decided a few weeks before. She was doing this to express her appreciation for all the hard work I do, for showing up every day, and giving it my all for so many years.

I was speechless. And my heart swelled with even *more* gratitude and appreciation.

My letter had not been an attempt to manipulate her towards this outcome. In truth, I hadn't felt valued at my work by my co-workers or my boss. Quite the opposite. I had felt underappreciated for the entire four years I had been working there, spending a lot of time behind closed doors, complaining and bitching about how ungrateful the business was for my hard work, and about how much I put in and never felt like I got anything back.

This was also how I had felt at every job prior. Clearly something wasn't working for me and clearly I was the common thread between all my work problems. I had to make the change from within. I had to become that which I wanted to experience more of in my life and my work. I was the missing link between the life I wanted to live and the life I was actually living.

The moment I became the *embodiment* of that which I wanted to experience more of, it showed up for me without me begging for it, complaining about it and without any real effort on my part. I *embodied* that which I wanted to experience more of in the world—in this case appreciation and gratitude.

The Law of Attraction governs all aspects of the world. When you embody any specific qualities, the Universe has no choice but to reflect those qualities back to you through your outside world. That which is like unto itself is drawn. All cooperative components come together to give you the exact experience you are emitting out into the world.

Looking at the world around you and complaining that it doesn't match what you want puts you in a place of powerlessness.

In my last brief relationship, I desperately wanted to find and inhabit my true sexual self. It's a part of myself I'd abandoned in past relationships—looking only to please my man as a diversion to voicing what I desired. I spent a lot of time reading books, taking courses, and practicing manifestation techniques to attract the partner I wanted into my life.

In every vision and dream I created in my mind we were having amazing, breathtaking, toe curling, body-levitating *sex*. In my vision it was magical.

Finally, after waiting around for what felt like forever, a new man showed up in my life. He was the closest thing to a healthy relationship I'd ever experienced in real life. I smiled inside with the realization that a person such as I'd been imagining actually existed.

It didn't take long after we met to start talking sex, something that always made me feel a little uncomfortable but made my stomach flip with excitement at the same time. *Great*, I thought to myself, *he's going to also be the one to crack me open sexually*!

While it was pleasing at first, a couple months passed by and the act became more infrequent, and I found myself feeling less and less involved every time. It wasn't the deep, bonded and intimate connection I'd longed for and I felt frustrated that *he* wasn't making it such. I was angry that he wasn't pushing me to be the feminine, sexual goddess I *felt like* on the inside.

It didn't take long for this situation to lead into the demise of our short-lived relationship. I blamed myself. I blamed him. I hated myself. I hated him.

Why hadn't he stepped up and guided me into discovering the sexual woman I knew I was? I mean, there were times when he attempted to do so through spanking, hair pulling and the rest. But this wasn't what I was craving. I wanted a deep connection to my own body and to God through my sexual acts with a loving leading partner. That's what I was craving! I knew who I wanted to be in my sexual relationship, but for some reason, the being I wanted to be and who I was presenting myself as, weren't in sync.

The one thing I desired most in my life and in my relationship was the one thing that had torn it apart. At least this is how I saw it in my mind at the time. I'd expected this person to show up and draw out of me the qualities I was dying to express within myself but had kept mostly buried away until now. I wanted our connection to allow me to step fully into my own sexuality, understanding my body, what pleased it, and finally being able to climax with an actual partner and not just via my own self-stimulation.

I reacted by throwing myself into everything that would express my sexuality and femininity more openly. When I take action, I tend to go full out! I enrolled myself in multiple pole dancing classes, dressed myself up in sexy lingerie and danced around my bedroom, and stared at myself in the mirror. I also bought a bunch of fancy rubber toys, hand restraints, and blindfolds. I started masturbating regularly, even when I didn't really feel like it. I walked around my house naked and I slept naked, which ended my habit of sleeping in full sweatpants and a hoodie.

I began freeing myself.

At first I was doing it because I wanted to be accepted. I had felt like this man had rejected me for not being an overly sexual woman and so initially I tried to become what I thought he had wanted but I was lacking.

The truth was that it had nothing to do with him. Nothing at all. But it had *everything* to do with me.

I felt rejected by him for lacking these qualities because I was an extremely sexual woman, feminine to the core, yet I was *denying* this in myself. I was tucking it away in a closet—unexpressed. I was waiting for someone to give me permission to let this person out. In reality, the only person's permission I needed all along was my own. And it took a man I cared about walking away from me for me to figure that out. Now I know and understand that we indeed had a Divine Contract, which helped me learn exactly this. Now, I'm grateful for the experience and what it taught me.

As I dove into the exploration of my sexuality, I discovered that I *love* dancing in an erotic, feminine way. I love it so much. I love swaying and moving my hips slowly and rhythmically. I learned that my craving for slow deep penetration was actually me trying to connect spiritually to my partner, myself, and God.

This was something I'd been ridiculed for in this short-lived relationship. He'd expressed how he liked it rough, and I in turn had became self-conscious.

It seemed neither of us were clearly communicating what we desired sexually and thus the discord grew between us.

I wanted to be made love to. I wanted to be opened, cherished, and penetrated to my soul. This was what turned me on, and all it took was me owning that this was what felt good to me.

Then I came across the world of Tantric sex and began participating in events and workshops. They literally changed my life for the better. I felt like the skies and clouds had parted and I was able to see the light. Ahhhh... There were other people doing it the way I was doing it, I just didn't have a word for it. I didn't know there was an actual *practice* of this kind of sex I was so deeply craving. I had no idea. I was just following the natural inclinations of my body and that's where it led me.

I embodied the quality I wanted in my life. No one was going to come along and open me into being who I wanted to be, open me into becoming the sexual woman I felt like but refused to express. No one could do this for me but me. I had to own it. I had to express it. I had to embody it.

And when I did, worlds opened up. Miracles started occurring. I felt things within my body and my pussy I'd never felt before. I've become, and continue to become the woman I wanted a man to make me into.

I was just radically confused about how to get there. I continue to learn and grow and express this side of myself in different ways.

For years I'd admired, yet felt uncomfortable, around openly sexual women—the ones who looked radiant in their bodies no matter their size, who openly asked for what they wanted and knew their bodies well enough to know what pleased them and turned them on, the ones who could enter a room and ooze grace all over it, and the ones who were comfortable in their own skin and comfortable being a woman. I envied them. I would stare at them. Sometimes I even got mad at them, questioning who they thought they were to "demand" all this attention.

What I didn't understand was that I both loved and resisted them because I was seeing within them, aspects of who I actually was, but refusing to let shine through. I was refusing the call to harness it. When I did, worlds opened up.

It's a beautiful feeling to become the person who was once just a vision in your imagination. To actually experience and feel the things you thought could only come to you through someone else serving them. It really, really is a beautiful thing.

Embodiment is more than just looking at the qualities within other people and the things that turn you on in the world with admiration and inspiration— it's the taking of these qualities and demonstrating them within your own life.

It's the slowing down and *being* that which you've been *chasing*. It's the implementation of all the things you've understood intellectually, but haven't seen appear in your own life. It's the constant and consistent choice to show up and *be* that which you wish there was more of in the world.

Self Reflection Exercises

Take note of the answers to these questions:

- What do you wish the world had more of?

- What do you wish you saw more of when you are out and about running your errands?

- What would have to manifest in the world around you for you to feel absolute happiness and bliss?

- What would it look like?

Think about it, describe it and write it down in *full* detail.

Okay, now since it would take *a lot* of effort, stress, and time to go around you and change every minute detail, person, and situation into what you wish they could be, instead dissect the simple qualities that this ideal image is holding.

- What are those qualities within it that you could start being, doing, and saying now?

- Do you wish people in your family or work environment appreciated you more?

- Who then, in *your* life, can you start expressing more appreciation towards? These can be people you don't know personally but have short encounters with in stores, coffee shops, gyms, or yoga classes. Or perhaps the person who absolutely triggers you the most and makes you feel totally bat shit crazy in their presence.

Chapter 14:

Layer 7 – Be Your Fucking Self!

Have you ever examined a snowflake? The intricate webbing forms a beautiful little piece of artwork tiny enough to fit on the nail of your pinky finger. Did you know that no two snowflakes in the entire world that have ever fallen or that will ever fall are identical? Not one from a thousand years ago and not one from the winter past. They're all different, unique to themselves. What a magnificent unlimited Universe we must live in to be able to produce endless snowflake designs!

Like snowflakes, every one of *us* is unique from one another in our physical form. We all emanate from the same Source, yet we're all gloriously individualized projections of this Source Energy, focused in this time-space reality to be and do only what we're able to do and be. There's no one identical to you. Not even identical twins are the same!

How crazy and cool is that? *No* two people in the entire frickin' world who have ever existed or whoever will exist are or will be the same!

Why is this so important?

It's all too easy to feel insignificant in this lifetime, and to feel like there's someone out there already doing it bigger, better, and more efficiently than you are. It's easy to feel that you could never compare to these people, and the truth is, you *can't* because you're entirely magnificent in your own right.

You aren't like them, and even while you might feel like you have a similar message to communicate, the way you communicate it is completely individualized. Different people will resonate with you than they might with someone else who's spreading a similar message or teaching. This is because they need to hear it in only the way *you* can share. Like the snow-flakes, your voice is unique and the way in which you deliver your message and what's important to you will be different to others even when it feels like the same message.

The reality is that it usually *is* the same message because in Spirit we all resonate the same truth. We're all love. We all emanate from the same source. It's the contradictions in life that we *physically* manifest differently, only to be exactly the same underneath, abiding by the same Universal laws and principles articulated in a thousand different tongues.

A couple of months ago I went to a concert at a local venue to see a rap artist whose music I've loved for a long time. After the concert I had the opportunity to meet the artist and spend some time hanging out with his crew, including his producer, DJ, and manager. It was an interesting experience that I appreciated for what it was. As I mentioned my fascination with the lifestyle of celebrities and famous people earlier, I was deeply intrigued by these men and their way of life.

As I often do, I found myself in a deep conversation with the producer about... well... LIFE! There's a part of me that finds famous and successful people's lifestyles to be fascinating. I love finding out about them because they don't fit into the norm. I envy them because, like them, I want to live a life I create on my own terms, and set my own schedule, timetable and more.

I don't remember the exact context of that portion of the conversation, but we were discussing how I coach people and help them through areas where they feel stuck. Somewhere in explaining this, I stated that, "In truth, we're all the same."

The producer looked at me puzzled, as if to say "What...?"

I replied to his unspoken words, but rather to the look on his face, which said, *We're not all the same.* He looked perplexed.

I quickly grasped we were communicating from different levels. It's obvious when I look around and spot differences in our physical appearances, the personas we adopt, and the things we acquire. I see we separate ourselves into hierarchies and by status, based on categorizing people on their perceived dollar value and how much they earn each year. We try to pin down who a person is by the car they drive, the career titles they hold, skin and hair color, the clothes they wear, and the way they carry themselves.

Our outer affections are merely our shell—the outer layer of skin-deep traits that protect the deeper parts of us. We're all Spirit, encased temporarily in human bodies, which are nothing more than our flesh vehicles for our time on this planet. They're the transitory part of us that age and will eventually die.

What I meant when I said to this man that, "In truth, we're all the same," was that underneath all the layers of identity we've built up, we are *one*. When everything's stripped away, we all desire love more than anything else. We desire to feel happy, free, and accepted over any superficially acquired title or image we give ourselves. In truth, all these are is the mani-festation of us seeking acceptance and love, somehow believing we can prove ourselves worthy to another in order to gain their love.

We are, in fact, already deserving of love, happiness, and acceptance just for BEING.

In this interaction, he was speaking to the fact that we're all individuals. I see this as us all being indi-vidual expressions of the same Divine source energy!

For the first twenty years of my life, I tried to figure out who I had to be to get love, and who I needed to show up as to be accepted by the people I wanted to love me, as well as society. I looked around and observed what people, who I thought were being accepted by the world, were doing. Clearly, in my mind, they knew something I didn't or they were just miraculously gifted with some kind of innate quality that automatically gave them a free pass into acceptance. I genuinely thought these people were just luckier than I was and that I was born with some disadvantage, having to exert great amounts of energy to have people love and accept me while the other "Gifted Ones" just did it naturally.

After twenty-four years I couldn't take it anymore. The entire structure that I called my life, and which had been built on weak foundations, was now crum-bling around me. I felt like I was breaking. Everything

I forced myself to identify with was being ripped away from me. I felt like I was losing everything.

Some people go through a life crisis where they lose external things like their marriage, relationship, job, house, pet, or other. For me, the crisis was internal.

It was as if there was a lioness inside of me, trapped in a cage, pacing back and forth, roaring and clawing to be let free. She was done with being caged up and forced into silence and submission. Instead, my lioness was messy, unpredictable, and relentless. I had no idea what would happen if I let her loose.

As my lioness grew more and more frustrated and less and less tolerant of being hidden away, she threatened to break free. I tried to hold her back. I resisted. I did anything not to *reveal* myself.

But my lioness did come out and I'm free now. I don't know how I survived so many years trapped away, hidden, diluting myself, so I wouldn't be "too much" for people to handle or judged.

It didn't happen overnight. I did it in gradual and consistent shifts in how I showed up, how I spent my time and with whom I spent it, and in the things, people, and situations I *let go*.

The more I shifted, the closer I could feel myself getting to who I knew I really was. It was still scary as shit, and I stumbled and fell along the way. But each time I'd get up, scraped knees and all, to take another step forward, I allowed my internal guidance to light the path even when I could only see a few feet in front of me.

Once in a while I'd break free from the gentle hands of my inner guidance, convincing myself I could figure it out better on my own by heading down a different road. But then I recognized I was abandoning my inner self. The realization happens so much quicker now because I can tell how I *feel*. When I've strayed from the path of my heart and truth of who I *really* am it begins to feels funky. It feels off. It feels foreign.

When your true self is trapped in a cage, you don't actually get the love you desire. You don't get the outcome you're pursuing even when you think you're stepping meticulously in the right direction. You don't get the acceptance and you don't get the fulfillment. It can't happen when you're masking yourself to the world. The love you do end up receiving won't feel genuine because you can feel deep within your heart, even if you can't vocalize it, that people are falling in love with who you choose to show up as and not *who you really are*. People simply can't love you for who you are if you don't show them and allow them to *see* the real you!

So why is it that many of us struggle to just be what we already are? Why is that? This is a mystery that has perplexed me for years. As I reveal who I am more and more, I'm awakened to the truth and see beyond the masks of others into who *they* really are. I hear the words they speak and perceive the shell they construct, and I just don't buy it.

It's only been through opening up and expressing my true self to the world that I'm able to see into the truth of others as I interact with them. The golden qualities dwelling within their soul jump out and smile at me—a warm beam of light. The qualities that might seem off or quirky about them are the very things I fall in love with about them... it's their *Is-ness*!

I briefly see their flaws, triggers, and ego mentalities, but it's fast becoming only a brief experience. Their claws and daggers come out, and I in turn respond with the same via my default defense system. But just as quickly as my protective mechanism is unleashed, I realize what I'm doing. I can see I'm triggered by them, and that my ego feels attacked by their ego. Now when I recognize this pattern I can put away my boxing gloves more quickly, and see what parts of me are really me, what parts of them are really them, and what parts are masks coming up to protect us both. That's really all I see the masks we put up as—a protection mechanism keeping us safe from the judgments and ridicules of the outside world.

When I start seeing a person only as their exterior mask, I know it's a cue to check in with myself to see where I'm living in my own ego and how I've waivered from my truth. The world is my mirror after all, and I cannot observe in another what I don't also observe within myself.

Just the other day I had an incident at work that perfectly demonstrates what I'm talking about. It was a busy Saturday and I was at the salon doing clients' hair. I discovered one of my long time clients had booked in with another stylist rather than me. I had a cancellation during the time and so I asked our receptionist to call her and let her know I could see her now. The receptionist followed through with the request, but the client didn't respond in the way I'd anticipated. This stylist had cut my client's hair the previous time when I'd been unavailable and my client had decided to rebook with her again.

It was a blow. A hard blow to my ego *and* my heart, and I felt it hard in the pit of my stomach. Crazy how such a simple and seemingly small thing can rip open our core wound—my own core wound being abandonment. I felt abandoned by my client and on a subtler level, I felt abandoned by my co-worker.

Later that day, I went up to our receptionist and snapped at her for charging this client a lower rate than she is usually charged. This was the same client whose hair I hadn't even cut that day! Yet, I became self-righteous, and unleashed on our dear receptionist.

I left the salon that evening, went home and felt *something* nagging inside of me. Rather than turning to food or busying myself all night to avoid confrontation with the said *something,* I stopped, pulled out a pen and started scrawling on an empty journal page. Exploring how I felt through the words I was scribbling across the crisp page, gave me a new depth of clarity. I felt guilty. Ashamed. *Bad.* I didn't like how I'd reacted earlier that day.

Rather than brushing this feeling aside, I picked up my phone and texted the receptionist. I apologized for being rude and snappy with her earlier in the day. I wanted to take it a step further though by explaining to her I was feeling insecure and hurt that my client had chosen to see someone else.

Vulnerability.

I admitted to someone else that I was feeling hurt and abandoned rather than defaulting to my regular position of defense and justification. It felt scary as hell, but I knew it was going to change a deep seeded pattern and, in doing so, I would also set myself free.

When my co-worker responded, she was more than understanding, kind and compassionate towards me, emphasizing that, "It can't be breezy *every* day, right?"

And right she was. The ups and downs, the ebb and flow, they're all a part of the journey. Her simple statement provided me with a gentle reminder of this.

What *Is* Your Truth?

Your truth is yours alone, dying to break free and express itself. It's not something that has to be found or discovered, polished or perfected. It's whole and complete as it is. It's within you whether you've chosen to honor and reveal it or not.

It's there.

It's always been there and always will be there. It's unique to you and no one else.

You were purposefully put here with this specific truth for good reason. No one can rob you of your truth. No one. Not society. Not your family and parents. Not your friends. Not your partner or your tribe. No one. You can only use them as reasons to *resist* your truth. This is, however, a made up perception in your mind.

Your truth is what makes you, **YOU**! There are no concise words to describe exactly what that is. There's no definite shape and structure that it follows. It has no beginning and no end. It's every piece of you, woven into every cell of your body, laced into every thought that runs through your mind and every emotion that floods your heart.

You can spend your entire life denying it, suffocating and pushing it down with endless amounts of drugs, alcohol, sex, food, and shopping, running around endlessly in the rat race in an attempt not to face it. Even so, it'll continue to whisper to you until your death. It might even explode into some catastrophic event in your life in a plea for your attention to be heard and expressed. Even when it does this, it's for your best interest and your highest good. It'll only actually *get* to this point if you ignore it. But don't let it be a tragedy or catastrophe that wakes you up.

You can simply choose to tune in, and to get quiet enough to hear what's been there all along, only waiting for you to stop running away from its message.

How to Uncover Your Truth

It's not as difficult as you might think to uncover your truth. It doesn't have to be a long road full of struggle and pain. Instead you can choose to walk down the path with ease and grace.

I experienced a great deal of internal conflict and hesitation before I finally took my first steps down the road of grace, ultimately realizing that this was the fastest road to where I wanted to get to all along.

I want to help you make the bold choice to walk down this road no matter *where* your entry point is. What you've read may be completely new information to you. In fact, the life you're currently living may not be resonating with what you truly want it to be. Or perhaps you're already in the middle of making massive life changes. It's really never too early and never too late. But do know, that even if things are seemingly going well and you still feel this tiny inner buzz that something is slightly *off*, then that's your call to live your truth and to bring it to life.

Where Do You Go From Here?

You've woken up, been shaken up a little bit (or maybe a lot!), and now want to live what feels like your truth. The only problem is you have no idea where to begin!

Sometimes it can feel very overwhelming if you realize your entire life is structured around the various masks you've been wearing for many years that hide and protect your truth. It can feel like a rewiring of your whole existence is necessary in order to get you back on track from how far you've strayed. While this might be true right now... that's *okay*.

To accomplish those goals it becomes a matter of unlearning much of what you've learned up until this point. It takes a commitment to get curious.

Notice how I'm saying it requires *unlearning* not *changing*. That's because who you really *are* cannot be changed. Your Is-ness is who you are and we don't actually need to change you to reveal it. All you need to do is to uncover it and remove the masks you've been consciously or subconsciously wearing, which were created when the world attempted to mold you into its version of who it wanted you to be. This was done through your schooling system and man-made "laws." The only laws of truth are those of the Universe. Everything else must be checked at the door.

It's time to open your mind to a fresh way of living, thinking and being. It doesn't have to be difficult. In fact, it shouldn't be. Go into this with the exact intention that it'll be simple, harmonious, and will unfold with ease and grace. The only pain you'll feel is in dealing with the death of the things you *think* define you. Release the identities that aren't serving you anymore. If you're still clinging desperately to those things then it's a sure sign you need to let them go.

A lot of us have spent a long time adapting and molding ourselves to be someone we're not, and this has become routine and "normal" for us. Living disconnected from peace is the way we walk through every day. Changing to fit what the world expects from us has become something we've accepted as "just the way it is."

I'm here to tell you this isn't the way it has to be, and that you can easily unlearn and let go of your old ways of thinking in order to uncover and reveal the juiciest version of yourself that's been conditioned to hide. However, this can only happen if you will allow it. We've become so accustomed to living a lie that we believe it's difficult to uncover our own truth. The reality is it actually requires extreme measures to keep who we really are at bay!

Our mainstream world doesn't want you to unleash your authentic self unless it fits into the allotted categories pre-determined by the whole. *Different* scares people. Fear is at the base of judgment, especially if it's a reaction to something different than what others think to be successful and efficient or something that goes against the grain. Society wants you to fit in and be as it tells you that you should be.

The problem is we aren't meant to fit into the same generic blueprint, outlined in the black and white of how we're *supposed* to live our lives, forcing us to choose labels and generalizations about who we are.

Somewhere along the way, many of us got the idea that we must ask for someone else's permission to do or become what we want to. This manifests in many different ways for people.

A lot of my life was spent waiting for evidence or confirmation that it was okay to be who I was. I was waiting for permission. It's almost as if when I observed someone else living what I felt was similar to my truth, I would take this as the go-ahead for me to show that part of myself. I didn't realize at the time that all I had to do was just be who I *felt* I was in the first place.

That's the thing! Just the fact that you feel a certain way or see things a certain way or believe certain things *is* confirmation that these facets or qualities of you are acceptable to express. *Even* if no one else in history has spoken the words you long to speak, written the words you long to write, or become the person you long to become, it's still okay for you to do so.

Someone else doing it isn't the permission you require! What *is* required is your *own* permission and you can choose to give yourself this permission starting *right now*.

My need to gain permission to be myself from an outside source manifested in my early dating life. When some of my dates would express something that resonated with me, I'd find myself exclaiming, "Yes!" in agreement. Oftentimes these would be ideas about spirituality, traveling, and worldly views and values.

I'd feel myself rejoicing that I'd finally found my match, my partner, the person who lived the same way I did! Yet shortly after I'd find myself perplexed and confused as to why they weren't pursuing things further with me, as well as why I was more interested in them than they were in me. How could we feel the same way about so many major life things and they *not* want to move things forward with me even if it was just a second date?

The thing was though—I wasn't actually *expressing* the inner *truths* we aligned on. I recognized aspects of myself in these men, which I then took as permission to "come out of the closet" so to speak even though I wasn't actually living them in my own life. My dates, however, weren't observing who I felt like and was sheltering away on the inside. They were only seeing the person I presented on our date night, even if this person wasn't who I really felt I was at my core. People don't have laser sight, seeing past our persona, especially not on a first date! It's as if by them expressing views and values that resonated with my truest self, I was given permission to *also* express these parts of myself. In truth, I only needed my own permission.

I would be enveloped by utter disappointment and sadness when these men wouldn't pursue me further, but I began to understand the deeper root of my sadness came from the place within me that knew I was rejecting myself. The qualities I saw and loved in these men were the very qualities within my deepest core truth that lay dormant and unexpressed. The devastation I felt from not being accepted by these men was really the manifestation of my own inability to accept myself.

Another example of this dynamic is the one I presented in a previous chapter when I talked about expressing my sexuality and waiting for my partner to draw these aspects out of me rather than allowing myself to just embody them.

When these parts of ourselves are expressed we attract people who have the same vibrational match. On the other hand, when we attract people into our lives that reject those parts of us, it's symbolic of our own rejection of the same aspects of ourselves. This is a great opportunity to use the people in your life as a mirror to see what parts of yourself you're rejecting that could come into a more expressed version.

Self Reflection Exercises

Think of an interaction with someone, be it a date or anyone else in your life, where he or she expressed an opinion or value that had you silently or out loud shouting *YES!*

- What specific opinion or value was being expressed?

- Take a moment to be really honest with yourself, and then ask if this is an opinion or value that you've been actively expressing in your own life?

- If it's not, then what are ways you can more consciously express this truth that resonates with you in your own life?

- Write it down!

Is there something that you've always wanted to try or that you've always *felt* interested in, but haven't actively become involved with?

- What is this thing?

- How can you take action to make it a part of your life, expressing it rather than keeping it as something that lays dormant within you?

- Write it down!

Have you been waiting for someone's permission?

- Who's this person? Is it a specific person or is it society's permission?

- What have you held back on expressing because you were waiting for this person's permission?

- Why have you been waiting for this person's permission?

- Take a moment and make a conscious decision to drop the need for this person's permission and make an intention *right now* to give *yourself permission.*

- Write down what you're giving yourself permission to be and express!

Chapter 15:

What Living Your Truth Actually Looks Like – Knowledge In Action

It's all fine and dandy to follow your heart and truth when that path is paved by society, especially when it falls into what the crowd is doing, doesn't go against the grain, and goes under the radar of the masses. By saying that, I'm also presupposing that if you're reading this book, you don't fall into the category of being one of those people. In all likelihood, you've always felt like you were something *more* than what you saw when you looked around. At the same time, you might have felt like a total freak, as if you don't belong on planet Earth. You feel alone. Abandoned. You couldn't be bothered to participate in the usual conversations or activities that others around you seem so caught up in. No, there's always been a feeling of something *bigger* inside of you. You also felt as if you had something missing. A mission. A purpose. A calling towards something greater than yourself. You can barely put words to it, but you know it's there because you can feel it pumping through every cell of your body. Nor can you see it as a separate entity because it's so ingrained in you.

You've probably spent your entire life assuming that every person on the planet feels exactly the same way you do, and that you're all suffering, suffocating and dying from the inside out, crushing or smothering the message your entire being begs to share.

Not everyone feels this way.

But you do. You definitely do.

I have good news for you. You *were* born for something more—a Divine assignment. A mission you came forth onto the Earth to fulfill. And the very reason you've felt so suffocated is because you haven't been living out this mission.

There's no one to tell you what your mission is because it's completely unique and individualized to you. In fact, your entire life has been shaped and crafted around this personal mission.

You're a light worker—a bearer of the light. You've been sent here to help uplift the others living in harsh conditions within the world. Everything you've ever felt within you is truth. It's your truth. It's why you were born on this planet during this particular time. You very well might not even be able to put a finger on what it is you're here to do or how you go about doing it, but you can feel it. You can feel it nagging at you somewhere from deep within—deeper than the pit of your physical stomach and into the depths of your soul body.

People who live their truth and their personal message of light and love, leave no telltale signs or characteristics that others can observe and replicate. However, I want to help you find some clues from the inside out to help you discover and start to really live your truth.

There are three keys that'll help you know how deeply you are living your truth.

1. **You'll know by how you *feel*.**

Most people don't take the time to stop and observe how they feel within their bodies and emotions. Western culture has programed us to run on autopilot. We scramble to get things done, as well as to acquire financial and material wealth, not realizing that in the midst of these pursuits we lose all emotional richness.

Emotional richness is the key to living the life of your dreams. It's the key to living the purpose you came forth to fulfill. It can be, and only will be, found in how *you feel*. These are the feelings you can't fake. You can drown them out with drugs, alcohol, food, sugar, caffeine, business and an over-packed schedule, but underneath all of those surface suppressers, they still remain lingering. You can feel incredibly uncertain, as if your whole world might fall apart if you're to release these feelings bubbling below the surface.

So here you are living the *comfortable* life you've created for yourself, keeping your truth beneath the surface and the deep emotional richness you actually crave at bay. Yet something's missing. This something can often feel big, as if a part of your soul feels like it's burning up and dying every day you continue trekking through your so called "normal" life.

This is how I felt when I was doing hair full time, going to work every day and pretending that was all I desired out of life. I was always wondering what the missing piece was. I searched for it, even travelling across the world numerous times only to return home empty-handed and empty-hearted. The puzzle piece appeared to have been lost yet all the while it was *inside* of me.

It was only when I started tuning into my emotions, and I mean really, *really* tuning into them, that I put a finger on what my truth was. It was in this that I finally realized my truth wasn't an outward job, career, relationship, look or image. It wasn't the books I published, the clients I mentored, or the people I inspired. It was none of those things. They were *byproducts* of living my purpose.

By cultivating the *feelings* I want to feel from within, and generating my own emotional richness, it's only then that outside circumstances can manifest. In turn, they align with the core internal feelings I've connected to within myself.

In the early days, while I understood this in theory, I really wasn't living it. I would decide in my mind the feelings I wanted to feel and then set forth the intention of making them a part of my life. Yet, I would never actually take the time to sink into them or make a real commitment to experiencing them.

It was only when I made a pledge to myself to feel those feelings before the external evidence would show up that I found myself on track. After that, things started to effortlessly fall into place, unfolding with ease and grace.

Whereas previously I was chasing the life I wanted by getting the *things* I thought I desired through forceful action, I was now generating the emotional richness I wanted to experience. And by allowing that, the outside stuff started to shift, manifest and be pulled towards me without any struggle or over exertion on my part. Which leads me to the next key in living in alignment with your truth...

2. **You'll know by how much *flow* is showing up in your life.**

Flow. What's flow?

Flow is when things start moving, shifting and showing up in your life that seem beyond perfect for what you could have planned for yourself.

It's the synchronicities. The "coincidences"—the people, the places, the circumstances. The most perfect moment at the most perfect time with the most perfect person. It happens with little to no actual effort on your part, rather, you just find yourself smack dab in the middle of a scenario you couldn't have hand-crafted better yourself. The beautiful news is that it's not up to you to have to single-handedly shape the moments and circumstances of your own life. That's the Universe's job. I assure you the Universe is much more adept at this than you ever could be on your own!

I want to describe to you a story of flow and synchronicity that just very recently unfolded within my own life.

I'd just returned home from a month's stint of traveling to Peru, Bali and Thailand to a depleted savings account and my priorities reorganized. I wanted to make a change to how I handled my finances while simultaneously setting the intent to bring more people into my life to whom I felt greater love and connection.

One afternoon, an idea popped into my head to write a Facebook post, advertising that I was renting out the spare room in my home. It wasn't a decision I struggled with or even put much thought into—it just popped into my mind and I followed through.

A couple of days later, a friend who I dance with, private messaged me to let me know her friend was interested in my place and if she could pass along my contact info.

"Absolutely!" I replied.

Another couple of days later, the friend of my friend called me wanting to set up an appointment to come by, see the house and meet me. Instantly, I loved her energy over the phone and felt excited about the prospect.

To make a long story short, she came over the following week and we spent almost an hour chatting about our lifestyles, how we spent our time and what our passions, desires and living styles were. We just *clicked*. There really was no other word for it. We seemed to share the same core values and ethics while also possessing just the right amount of difference in our interests and personal lives.

Before she left, we began discussing where to put the furniture she wanted to keep, what of mine I wanted to keep and throw out, and how our living dynamic would work.

She showed up with no more effort on my end than a Facebook status. There were no endless hours of calling references and interviewing potentials. Instead she seemed like the perfect fit who just landed on my doorstep at the perfect moment. The synchronicity of finding a roommate without struggle was an indication that I was living in flow with what was the *next right step for me*.

This is flow state. This is when things in your life just move in harmony with you and everything else. These states are the Universe working with you and in your favor, conspiring to make your dreams a reality.

These synchronicities aren't coincidental. Quite the contrary, in fact. They are a direct result of you living your truth. You'll know how close to your truth you are living when outside circumstances line up in perfect order without you meticulously controlling them.

3. **You will know by the amount of *ease* present in your life.**

When ease shows up in your life it naturally follows your state of flow. They go hand in hand.

Ease is what I like to call major results with minimal effort. Indeed, the little effort you do exert is being exerting in the proper way.

Without tuning into your *real honest* feelings, everything you undertake will feel like a giant mountain you need to scale. You'll begin the climb and then just before you reach the peak you'll feel yourself starting to fall.

When you're in a state of living your truth, outer circumstances that previously felt impossible to create, begin manifesting around you. This is the outward manifestation of the internal feelings you've been generating. Do you see where your job lies and where the work of the Universe lies?

Somewhere along the way we got confused as to whose job title was what, and we took on far more than we were ever required to do. Why would we want to take on more than we need to when we can live the life we *dream* of with ease and grace? Because deep down, beneath the dream, what you're really craving is the feeling you think these *things* will provide for you. Isn't *that* what you're searching and striving for?

And wouldn't it be amazing to *have* those feelings pulsating through every cell of your body on a daily basis and as a result of allowing them to flow freely through you? Wouldn't it be incredible if all the outer *things* you thought would make you happier show up anyway with ease and grace, as nothing more than a result of the internal environment you've created for yourself?

HA! It's more bloody brilliant than we could ever imagine! It's perfection!

We've been taught to work within an ineffective model. But I want you to inquire—did the people who taught you how the world worked, live out *their* dreams? Did they fulfill their deepest heart yearnings during their lives?

If they lived anything less than this, I would question how rich their lives have been, and also ask how much of their philosophies you've allowed to creep into your own life.

You now know you can be more of who you truly are or you wouldn't be here right now in this moment, reading this book. This book found you for a reason. To remind you of what's already inside you, dying to be let out, to be expressed and brought to life. That is, a life beyond your mind's imaginings and manifested into the physical world.

This is why you were born. This is why you came here. You're right here right now exactly where you were meant to be in *this* very moment. Will you allow yourself to believe this? Will you allow yourself to be cocooned and nurtured by the beautiful Universe that's working in your favor every day and night to guide you along your truth's path, all the while bringing to you exactly what you need in every moment you need it, even when it shows up as the shattering of your world, total heartbreak, and utter tragedy? Could you, even for a moment, believe that it's all happening *for* you and not *to* you?

The entire Universe is conspiring in your favor, working to manifest your deepest dreams and desires into a reality. Remember that!

Conclusion

You contain within you the power to do, be and have absolutely everything you've ever dreamed about. The very fact that you've ever imagined it means the potential for it lives within you. It's who you are.

Everything everyone has ever told you is wrong with you is actually what's right with you. Your flaws are what make you so incredibly special! By releasing the voices embedded in your head that negate your dreams with roadblocks, you'll unlock the power within you to manifest those dreams. In fact, they aren't roadblocks at all. Rather, they *are* the road to your purpose and the life of your dreams.

Everything that has ever felt like it was standing in the way of you and your dreams is actually pointing you directly *toward* your dreams. That's the seemingly strange contradiction of this thing we call life. Your wounds provide you with the opportunity to heal yourself, heal your peers, and heal the world.

It's my greatest prayer that through the words on these pages you've recognized within yourself the spark that makes you your beautifully individualized self. It's my sincerest wish that you've been able to look at everything that has transpired in your life until this point and see it for what it was... exactly what you needed to experience and transform you into the person you are today. I hope you see that every obstacle life has placed in front of you is really an opportunity to usher you towards complete empowerment, fueling you to express everything that you've become.

It's my prayer that you see within yourself the absolutely perfect being you are. The perfect being you've always been in the midst of your greatest fuck-ups, as well as your most brilliant moments. None of these moments could ever undo your perfection.

It's my prayer that you further open up and show the world who you are to the absolute fullest expression, and that you never hold back what you know in the depth of your heart and soul to be true.

It's my prayer that through the honoring of your own truth and holding authentically to what feeds your soul that you give other people permission to do exactly the same for themselves.

It's my prayer that you love and accept this life in all of its entirety, cherishing and devouring every emotion that courses its way through the cells of your body.

It's my prayer that you find peace in every moment of bliss and joy.

It's my prayer that you find equal peace within every moment of challenge and sadness.

It's my prayer that you find absolute peace in *who you are*. Right here. Right now.

It's my prayer that you may approve of every part of yourself and that the only person's permission you ever seek is your own.

The End

Acknowledgments

Firstly, I want to thank *you*, my beloved reader, for picking up this book and answering the call from within. In doing so, you've unknowingly set into motion a chain of events, people and circumstances that will beautifully find their way to you and unfold in a way that's exactly meant for your expansion as a person and a soul. You've chosen to walk down the path of accepting, loving, and expressing who you truly are. For that, I commend you.

I want to thank my beautiful mother and sacred soul sister, Chris Sanderson. I know without a doubt that this isn't our first lifetime together and that we chose to be such a big part of each other's journey before incarnating. Thank you for allowing me the space and freedom to explore who I wanted to become, as well as live into who I am with minimal judgment. I'm in deep gratitude for the life you lived before me that gave me clarity on how I wanted to live. I'm so appreciative for your support as I continue to explore life.

It's important for me to extend genuine heartfelt appreciation to every person who has ever challenged me, pushed my buttons, and triggered the darkest parts of my being. I need not name each and every single person for there are far too many names and still more to come, I'm sure. Thank you for reflecting back to me the parts of myself that were crying out for my attention and healing. Without your mirror, I would still be hiding and denying these shadows inside myself.

So much love and gratitude to my amazing editor, Julie Ditrich, for fine-tuning this manuscript to exactly what I'd always imagined it could be. Your truthfulness and tough love were exactly what I, and this book, needed. Thank you for going above and beyond in guiding me through the process of publishing my first book.

I would like to send big hugs to my photographer Ruby Carino for shooting the cover image and bearing with me as we called it forth from my mind and into life. You are such a sweetheart.

Thank you to the staff and designers at Tellwell Publishing for helping bring this book into its physical published form.

Deepest thanks to all the thought leaders who have come before me, especially to all the women who had the courage to follow the path of their heart's desires. While many of these women I haven't met in person, I know we're deeply connected in spirit. Thank you for unknowingly giving me permission to follow my truth and light—Doreen Virtue, Esther and Jerry Hicks and Abraham, Rebecca Campbell, Regena Thomashauer "Mama Gena", Jaiya, and many others.

About the Author

Kat Trimarco is an Inner Beauty Stylist who helps women accept, love, and express who they truly are. She helps them return home to their truth, radiance, and deepest heart's desires. Her path was forged from the experiences and circumstances of her personal journey, which continues to refine and expand as she grows deeper into herself.

Kat is a Life Coach and Sex Coach who conducts private one-on-one coaching, hosts group work-shops, writes blogs, films video blogs, and presents motivational talks from the platform.

She currently resides in Edmonton, Alberta, Canada with her little Yorkie and best bud, Milo, where she continues to further her education and understand-ing of fulfilled and authentic living.

She can be contacted for private coaching via email at contact@KatTrimarco.com. For more information on her upcoming speaking events and workshops, please visit www.KatTrimarco.com where you can also sign up for her free newsletter for a weekly dose of inspiration.

CPSIA information can be obtained
at www.ICGtesting.com
Printed in the USA
LVOW08s1030090417
530146LV00001B/3/P